Habits

Build Powerful Destiny Changing
Habits

*(How to Create Smarter Habits That Adapt to Your
Day)*

Isaac Lohmann

Published By **Ryan Princeton**

Isaac Lohmann

Habits: Build Powerful Destiny Changing Habits (How to Create Smarter Habits That Adapt to Your Day)

ISBN   978-1-77485-765-6

Legal & Disclaimer

information provided by this guide. This disclaimer applies to any damages or injury caused by the use and application, whether directly or indirectly, of any advice or information presented, whether for breach of contract, tort, negligence, personal injury, criminal intent, or under any other cause of action.

You agree to accept all risks of using the information presented inside this book. You need to consult a professional medical practitioner in order to ensure you are both able and healthy enough to participate in this program.

TABLE OF CONTENTS

Introduction

It's not obvious however; routines are something we develop by default. Every day we are in the same routines and follow the same routines and patterns However, did you realize that you could use this to your own advantage. In every aspect that you are in, the habits you develop affect the success of people when it comes to their work, as well as their relationships and the general life. If you asked entrepreneurs about their habits they'd inform them that these are the foundation of their success. This is the case throughout your life, starting from the moment you wake up all the way to going to your bed. Your habits are what you do however, the interesting thing is the fact that scientists have discovered that the amount of neurons actively supporting the habits of adults decreases rather than growing. They were puzzled by this , and when they investigated it further discovered that when the neurons aren't being employed they tend to shrink.

James Clear wrote a wonderful piece on this topic that was published in the Huffington Post and which clearly describes the process and has everything about habits. Your mental and physical performance depends on developing habits that inspire you to move your life in a positive way. If you don't drink enough fluids for instance it is common to become weak and dehydrated. If you're not aware of the surroundings and you don't pay attention, you can become emotionally tense and insecure. So, if you're trying to change the way you perceive the world and how you react to it, you must be aware of what your habits create a negative impact on your life.

The neural connections are essential to improve your performance. It is evident that when you don't paint pictures, the brain cells dealing with the artistic portion of your brain are less active than those who paint. In addition, he claims that babies have what he refers to as a"blank canvas"where everything is possible. Adults are limited by honing in on specific abilities that they recognize they excel at. They are more likely to ignore areas in which their individual strengths are not applicable and so the neurons get grouped into groups of limited groups that focus on the strengths and eliminate what they perceive to be weak points.

When you change your habits and attaching new ones to existing ones, you're on your way to opening the neuronal areas, and expanding the possibilities of possibilities you have. If you're not convinced this is the case then you have to read the content of this book, as you'll discover the way that habits are formed and how adding another habit onto one that is already in place will Improve your life in many ways you didn't think was possible. The possibility was always there however, you've limited it because you see the blank canvas as full of potential rather than empty and full of possibilities. Limit yourself when you think like this, but If you could incorporate your new ideas into the ones you already have, you'll be able to boost the activity of neuron cells in your brain, and reap the rewards.

This is known as habit stacking; however I prefer piggybacking since that's basically what you're doing. You tie the habit to something that you are able to do, and then it is a natural element of your daily life. When you continue doing this, your life gets better as does the array of possibilities you can open yourself to. At the end of this book, you'll have developed thirty new behaviors that transform your perspective on your life. Your life will be transformed within 30 days when you follow the guidelines within this publication. You'll also be able to examine your weaknesses and then build on these areas, keeping all the neurons in your brain active, and further developing them by opening your mind to possibilities. Your limitations are limited only by the thoughts you create. Change how you view life, then your outlook on life is likely to be transformed forever.

Chapter 1: A Look At Existing Habits

The chapter we are discussing will will take an examination of the everyday mundane things you perform every day in your life. It is necessary to grab a notepad and pen and allow yourself a half hour to record everything that is the routines that you perform without thinking about. If you'd rather to carry notes with you throughout the day? take note of the daily routines that you integrate into your daily routine. You might be wondering what type of habit you are incorporating you should be incorporating, but let's talk about.

After you have gotten out of your bed in the morning, what do typically do? It is likely that you will instinctively go to your slippers. You could use the restroom. You could visit the bathroom to brush your teeth. All of these are routines. Then, you can go to the kitchen and make coffee. It is possible to go out and look over your letter. You'll most likely dress up.

They are habits, and they can use to build onto new routines. It is important to list them in order to be utilized as piggybacks however, don't record the things you should do. Note down the things that you do. It's a differentiator in that, despite all the good intentions that are out there in this world, when the thing you've selected isn't already a routine and you fail, then you'll be in the wrong. It is essential to establish real routines and positive ones in order that you can utilize them as motivators to incorporate new routines. For instance, you might believe that exercising should be a part of your morning routine, but not have exercised because you had other things to be doing. If you are motivated more than routines, you shouldn't add these as they're not habits as of this moment in the present.

The next step you must create an outline of your practices that will make your life better. You already know what they are since you're living your life. Perhaps you don't have enough time to stay in contact with your friends or you smoke cigarettes too often. Maybe you aren't drinking enough water as often as you could. You might find yourself distracted and need to focus more. Make a list of your priorities and make sure to include the followingitems:

1. Socialize more

2. Take a moment of spiritual reflection

3. Relax more

4. Be friendlier

5. Stay healthier

6. Be more compassionate

I've written these to help you see using the information you have of your life what areas of your life must improve. It's crucial and crucial to be honest about yourself. Maybe you're not great with people and wish you were. If that's the case, you should add the habit of more socializing. Maybe you aren't aware of the spiritual aspect of life . If this is the case, then add the habit of spirituality. Perhaps you're stressed and constantly over-stressed. In this case, consider your relaxation routine. Maybe you're a bit aloof and think you're not liked by others. Include the"Be friendlier"habit. It is possible to break down these areas of routine into smaller, easier to manage habits later on but first you have to admit that your life isn't giving you enough satisfaction, since each one of them will include behaviors that can be added onto your existing habits to make life more fulfilling. Let's explore specific areas and demonstrate how to integrate 30 new habits into your routine for 30 days, and help them stick.It's your choice to decide how many of them you will introduce at any given time, but make the list and start to mark each day you follow these new practices. When you tag them to previous and established routines You are providing yourself with an opportunity to prompt you determine the best time you should introduce the new habit.

Chapter 2: Focuses On Your Relationships

This chapter we will deal how you interact with other people. Maybe you're too busy that you're not able to show others who are around you that you value their opinions and due to this, you are feeling unwelcome and not easily drawn into new relationships or to keep existing relationships active and alive. When you incorporate new habits to your daily routine, you can fix this, and it doesn't take much time in any way.

When/Before I start this routine, I'll do ...

In the initial couple of days, until it becomes routine it is important to keep track of what you're adding in order that it is a habit. If you practice it frequently enough, your brains will begin to recognize it as an everyday routine and you'll do it without considering it. In the meantime, take a look at your list of habits you already have and figure out how you can create an additional habit. For instance:

Day 1

Lunch - Eat Take a break for lunch

You can decide to incorporate an exercise routine prior to or following your lunch:

Make phone calls and eat lunch

Or

Have lunch and make a phone call

The health of your relationships depends on how you interact with other people and maybe you've been thinking that you are too busy to be concerned about these relationships. Making a quick phone call during lunchtime to a person you trust can aid in keeping friendships going.

New Habit 1: Make phone calls

Time you have taken from your day Time taken from your day: 5 minutes

The result is that you stay contact with friends and can keep in touch with friends.

Let's test another habit. Are you prone to the habit of discussing yourself? This is common for people who have difficulty to keep relationships going. Set a new aim. You can talk about it. So, you can add this habit anytime you're talking to people. The habit could involve attending work. Try this on Day 2.

In the office, say"hello" to everyone

If you go to work, Make an appropriate comment to someone.

New Habit 2. Give a nice compliment to someone

Time taken: 5 seconds

The result: goodwill and the capability to connect with others in a positive manner.

There is a chance that you are a regular of attending meetings. If you do, try making a habit of it into your meetings. You can do this either before or after, as we've demonstrated.

Attend a meeting, smile at people and try to be positive

If you go to a meeting, smile

The New Habit 3. Smile

Time taken: 2 seconds

The result: Body language can make an immense changes to your relationships.

smiles can win you friends and influence others positively when your smile is displayed in a timely manner.

It is time to examine your relationships and examine all of your habits and routines that are shared with others. Look for ways to develop the piggyback behavior that will take place in line with your normal routines. It must be tied to a practice you practice on a daily day basis without contemplating it in order to be effective. Make sure to add the new habit to the previous one on your list. You can tick it each time you accomplish it. It will be apparent that people appreciate your company more and that you're capable of getting more enjoyment out of your social activities by being conscious of how your behavior determines the rewards you receive from your friends. You can add great habits that help improve the quality of your friendships. Make up some of your personal. If you've had a truly enjoyable experience, think about how you made an impact and include this into your routines.

Chapter 3: Your Spiritual Challenge

A lot of people believe they don't have the enough time to consider spiritual issues. Most don't even realize what the term "spiritual" means. It's a feeling of happiness that comes from being in awe of something that lets you look beyond the surface. If you are able to see birds fly through skies, it can make you feel awestruck. When you view the rainbow, you could be reminded of an omnipotent power that is watching over the world. Or, when you look at the vivid red of the sunset, you could feel lost for words. These things can will make you a better and more joyful human being, yet if aren't willing to accept them, you'll never build your spirituality, and it's equally important as other aspects of your life.

Things that are linked to spirituality can be any thing. Let's give you an example.

You should get up and go to bed. You do it every day and you don't have to think about it.

We can now incorporate a spiritual practice; open the drapes and take note of the colors in the night sky.

Fourth Habit: Being aware of the color of the sky

Time taken: 1 second

Results It makes you feel more connected to your surroundings and with yourself.

There are a myriad of practices that will help you be more spiritual. I've listed them below, and you are able to choose which ones to integrate into your routine. Keep in mind that this isn't a race. It's a matter of adding another habit on top of an already existing. This doesn't necessarily mean an end-to-end goal or any other difficult to achieve. It's just about changing your routine by introducing a new routine.

Possibly beneficial habits that can add spirituality to your daily life

Take a break from thoughts and be aware for a while This means you should take a moment of calm during the storm. Be aware of what's happening around you and be awestruck by it. It is possible to integrate this into your routine of eating by taking the time to take in the flavors and textures of the food that you consume, allowing your mind a break.

The New Habit 5, Be Mindful

Time required: less than five minutes

The result is that you are more conscious as well as less likely have negative thoughts.

If your life is brimming with activity, the chances are that you're not able to sit for any amount of time to let your mind get caught up in the world around you. Meditation is a great way to do this, and doesn't need to take a lot of time. Instead of thinking about the day, you just think about the breaths you take, and then shut your eyes for a time. It is possible to meditate for only five minutes and let your mind look at your surroundings in brighter light and with more energy than you've had before, especially in the event that you establish it as a routine every day.

New Habit 6 Meditation

Time Spent: 5 minutes

The result: More clear thinking and the ability to perceive things more clearly.

Perhaps you commute home each evening and pass by a place that could be amazing. You could start an additional habit of driving home and stop to go swimming. (Or any other place that could be an inspiration). In doing this, you're taking your heart while allowing for the more spiritual part of your personality some room to shine.

New Habit 7: Stopping at an inspiring location

Time Spent: 15 minutes

The result: Any positive habit that bring you closer with nature can lead to feeling inspired and feeding your spirituality.

Spirituality doesn't necessarily mean attending the church. It could mean that to certain people. Lighting candles in a church is a matter of only a few seconds and can be very spiritual if done with sincerity. Making small changes to your routine that doesn't take up an excessive amount of time can be the most beneficial thing to your spiritual outlook. You'll be able to tell if they're beneficial since they inspire you to be more positive about your life. If they don't, you can try another until you discover the habits that allow faith to be a shining light. Spirituality is something that you feel within. Let your imagination fly and find the ways to grow this aspect of yourself.

Chapter 4: Finding Time To Relax

Play, rest and work all play an integral role in the enjoyment you get from your life. If all you've got been occupied by work, then you'll get bored. If you are a lazy person and don't have the desire to work then you'll are unmotivated. Thus, there needs to be a balance between these three aspects. The three elements of rest, work and play must be a component of your day-to-day routine since when you throw the balance out, you can be prone to anxiety on one hand, and detachment on the other, and neither are good approaches to the world. The next chapter discuss relaxation since If you wish to excel at what you do you must have certain portions of your time devoted to enjoying yourself and relaxing.

Take a look at your current habit list and think about the areas where you could incorporate some relaxation, and incorporate it into your daily routine. For instance, it might not be appropriate for you to an afternoon nap during the lunchtime at work, however it might be a good idea to bring a crossword game to the park in the afternoon. It is important to determine what activities allow you to unwind and stimulate your brain while having fun. Certain people love playing video games due to the fact they let them turn off their real life for a brief moment. Certain people love solving word puzzles or expanding their vocabulary. The thing we're aware of is that positive habits are effective in the long run, whereas introducing negative habits aren't beneficial. Whatever you choose to integrate into your daily routine that allows you relax will be positive for you.

Relaxing in a comfortable place to eat sandwiches instead of eating in a hurry will help you relax. Look over your routine and include things that could become routines that are simple to adopt and be a part of your daily life. It will also help you get the rest you need. Here are some ideas:

Your usual habit - Go to the subway

New Habit 8 is to be added - While you're on the subway, relax in the park

The things you do are creating positive energy for your day. It is possible to board the train at the same time each morning. What about replacing your negative thoughts about work by solving an answer to a crossword? What do you feel about reading a few pages from a great book? There are activities that stimulate your mind. Reading and puzzles are great examples of things that will help you relax. Perhaps you're an avid player. What better way to get games like Word Feud to your phone and check it out each day at a time for you to allow your mind be free from the monotony of your daily routine. Don't view it as something you can indulge in. Consider it as an essential aspect of living. Keep in mind that you require an equal amount of working, play and rest and rest can be found in the rest zone in your daily life, or in the playing area of your life.

I board the train for the train ride to work

New habit: Play games online using your mobile. It could be an online word game, backgammon or chess - whatever you'd like to play.

The New Habit 9 Introduce Fun

Time taken: 10 minutes

The result: You are less fatigued and your batteries are more energized

After you arrive home, you typically sit on the sofa and enjoy a movie. Start a new habit prior to when you start watching television:

A new habit The newspaper should be read in silence. Relax after a tiring day's work.

A New Habit: slowing down the pace of your life

Time taken: 15 minutes

Results: You don't go from one world to another one as soon as you return back home.

It is important to unwind and those who are stressed by work often do not consider this to be useful and aren't sure how to turn off. When you establish a routine prior to turning on the TV allows you to enjoy to have a moment of silence to unwind. What you do with your time of relaxation is entirely up to you, based on the circumstances. It is possible to have a playdate with your kids prior to turning on the television. It is also possible to relax with your pet. It's your responsibility to determine what habits are appropriate to your lifestyle however, they should permit you to relax. There are a lot of other possibilities. Check them out.

Chapter 5: Productivity In Work

There's a good chance that you find yourself overwhelmed by the volume of work you're required to do. Many people feel this way and it's normal. What they don't realize is that by changing small changes, they could be more productive and less stressed. What you should consider is the behaviors that cause your workload to be heavy and some of them could be harmful habits that can hinder your growth. Do you, for instance, allow you to be interrupted frequently? Do you constantly jump between tasks or do you try to be multi-tasking? Have you heard that researchers advise that focusing on a single task at a time ensures that you can finish it faster? The brain is not designed to multitask, and when you are doing that it takes more time to complete the tasks in front of you.

The most productive time of day in terms of thinking and logic are concerned it is in the early hours of the morning and right after having a light lunch. I recommend a light meal since while some people consume a large lunch but a full meal could make you tired and lethargic instead of energetic. So, if there are things that have to be completed, they should be given priority. This can help you discern when you require less interaction with others so that your concentration levels are higher. This can give you a lot of control over how much work you can accomplish. There are three types of work:

1. High priority - focus needed

2. Priority Medium - Activities that you can do when talking to colleagues

3. Low Priority Things that are simple to accomplish and less important

You can use colors to be able to identify what jobs you are doing and start a new routine every day:

Work hard as you normally do. You can now add another one:

The New Habit11: triage of Workload

The time required for this task 5 minutes

Results: You can finish your top jobs quicker and you'll be more productive.

When you begin to work you'll know what tasks are most important that require no interruption. You you can schedule them to give you more time to complete these tasks without being irritated by your colleagues. Let people know that you're in need of space to accomplish the job and then adopt an established routine.

Your usual routine is to start working.

The new routine is initiated before you get started at working.

The New Habit of 12: Let others be aware that you do not wish to interrupt them. Turn off your cell phone social networks, and all other interruptions.

Time taken: Three minutes

Results: You have more focused time to get through your top priorities which means that you won't need to let work pile over your desk and spiral way out of hand.

You are offered an assignment that you are aware that someone else is better at. Most of us hold onto these tasks because we're not a fan of delegating. But, it is important to keep in mind the fact that when someone else could handle it faster than you or have more information than you do, then delegation is a good idea. Therefore, the next time that you're gazing at an email that you know could be better handled through someone else you can delegate the task.

The old fashioned way of doing it is opening an email to discover it's beyond your capabilities or reach:

The New Habit of 13: Forward it directly to the person who you think will be able to do the job better.

Time was taken 2 seconds

The result: You are able to get along better with other people. You are more trustworthy and don't take time to do things you know that someone else will perform faster.

Workplace life isn't always stressful. Examine the habits you are currently practicing and make positive new ones that are related to your work environment and can make your day happier and productive. So, your work is reduced and you have more time to focus on the things that are essential. It's all about the way you work, and changing it by introducing new practices. If you change your habits you alter the attitudes of others too, since they react to the person you present yourself as and, with your new ways of being you will present positive for you.

Chapter 6: Habits Of Health Habits

For some , implementing healthy habits is a lot of effort. For instance are there many that have failed to lose weight? How many are you aware of who attempt to drink sufficient water, but fail? Are you considering quitting smoking cigarettes? The people who are looking to exercise usually begin with good intentions but then give up because they lack the time. All of these actions make up healthy practices. It is essential to incorporate healthy habits into your lifestyle in order to get the most enjoyment of living a full life. Here are some examples of practices can be incorporated into your daily routine that do not that demanding of effort.

New Habit 14 Take an ounce of water. Add it after any routine activity throughout the day.

Time taken: 2 minutes

The benefits are that your body will feel less dehydrated, and you experience less pain and aches due to.

Drink 8 glasses per day, however when you sip a glass of water and then add it after some of your routines each day and you slowly progress to the point of wanting for more. Patients suffering from ailments like fibromyalgia or mobility related diseases often don't realize the extent to which they're harming their bodies through not drinking water. It is possible to argue that coffee and tea are just water but they both are diuretics. This implies that the more water you consume the more you have to need to urinate, but your body won't conserve the liquid it requires. Drinking water is more beneficial because it gets to those areas in your body that are needed and makes muscles more elastic and less prone to inflammation.

What can you then do that will give you more exercise? Perhaps the phrase "exercise" appears like work. Imagine doing press-ups and you know that after a few repetitions minutes, you'll just quit. How about adding a bit of more walking to make it a habit? At the time you start your job each day:

The New Habit: Use the stairs instead of the elevator

Time taken: 2-3 minutes

Benefits: You experience an increase in even oxygen flow through your body. This is what makes you feel more energetic more.

What about coffee breaks? If you make a stop regularly to take a break, consider adding another habit that can help you feel better. Instead of having that cookie or cake after your morning coffee, consider this:

A New Habit for 16: Start eating fresh fruits

Time taken: One minute

Benefits: You'll receive lots of minerals and vitamins and need not need to stockpile carbs.

What do you think of the dinner? When you gather with your loved ones, do you sit back and relax during the dinner or do you eating to get it over with? Most people eat fast. Try this following your have sat down to your dinner:

A New Habit 17. Chew your food correctly and relish the flavors and tastes

Time required: Perhaps an additional five minutes

Benefits: The most important organ in your abdomen is your stomach. If you think it will handle food that is not digested and isn't chewed properly it is possible to suffer from constipation, cramps or trapped wind, as well as trapped air within your digestive tract. If you take the moment to chew food properly, you will not have these issues.

You can only determine which behaviors you're guilty of. If you smoke before eating Try separating yourself by changing your habit. You stand up every night after your dinner and immediately smoke cigarettes. You can try introducing the habit of this habit of smoking on the back shelf

The New Habit18: Take a tablet that replaces nicotine.

Time taken: 2 minutes

Benefits: You could be able to quit smoking cigarettes and add years to your life expectancy.

Your health is paramount. Check your own weaknesses and implement small changes that can help improve your diet, the quantity of exercise and getting rid of bad habits that affect your health. Drink plenty of water and feel healthier.

Chapter 7: Upping Your Empathy Levels

In the past, we've discussed 18 possible habits to change and offered you 30. The next chapter will deal by introducing some new behaviors that can help you become more content with yourself and people around you. Your levels of empathy have an important role in this. If you're not feeling empathy, this means your tolerance of other people is lower than that of those who have. Empathy refers to the ability to put yourself in another's shoes and look at the world through their eyes. Business executives are learning something known as Neuro Linguistic Programming, which helps them think about problems from different perspectives. This is like empathy. If you are aware of what a business will likely require to run its work efficiently, and you can give them that then you'll be able to increase the amount of sales. If you narrow your focus on your personal need to sell, you'll sell less. Being aware of other people's needs and understanding their motives and motivations to think about matters in a completely different approach to your own can let you see beyond your own expectations and make life simpler. If, for instance, you are prone to not paying attention to what others tell you, it is time to alter that behavior because people who are active listeners are able to learn a much better than people who are unable to pay attention.

Here are some practices you can implement into your routine, and then add them to your routine daily activities to make them integral to your identity and what you represent. People around you are essential to your existence. In the event that you choose to make your relationship to them negative, it will have a long-lasting negative impact.

When you've served your breakfast, you can introduce an entirely new routine:

The New Habit of 19: Pay attention to what others around you have to say

Time required: 15 minutes maximum

Benefit: You discover something about those you cherish and are able to respond to their needs more effectively. Parents who say they don't get their kids' point of view maybe they need to realize that they don't listen to them.

A New Habit 20 Call people and initiate the first contact

Time taken: 10 minutes

Benefit: You prove that you show a degree of respect for the person and they will see your character in a positive way.

New Habit 21: Help someone in need of assistance

Time Taken: 15 minutes

Benefit: Volunteerism can be used to make you feel like your life is purposeful.

A new habit 22 is to breathe deeply whenever things bother you.

Time taken: 2 minutes

Benefit: There could be some underlying reason why this person is causing you trouble and some of it could be attributable to you. Do not cause more problems by causing more stress because by doing that, your life gets more difficult.

A New Habit: Be observant of the world occasionally

Time taken: 2 minutes

Benefit: You'll learn to better understand other people and become an improved person through the process.

Do you understand how this is working? The new habits you create are relatively simple to integrate into your daily life. You must realize that each one is as simple as taking a single off, but should you attempt to put them all up and alter your personality this is a major issue and could easily be addressed through small, tiny changes known as habitsthat are introduced into your lifestyle that will take only a few minutes to adopt. I've compiled an additional list of possibilities of habits that you can incorporate into your daily life with no regard to the time that you've taken them and the advantages because these will be apparent to you once you have implemented the changes. You may appear to be an improved person, however what you're really doing is changing your basic way of life and becoming a more effective person. You'll feel more comfortable with yourself because of it, and you will be able to enhance your interactions with other people as a result.

Discuss it with a friend rather than talking to them about them/her instead of you.

Spend a few minutes volunteer - it will boost confidence in yourself and also helps others in the process.

Chapter 8: Habits Of The Home

Consider the activities you do at home and if the house is messy there is no need to be. Make the necessary changes and become more organized, and your life will be simpler. The last habit included within this guide will aid you in making your home a better space to live in:

The New Habit: Following your bathroom visit Change the toilet roll, if needed

The New Habit of 25 Following taking a shower, Hose off the shower area to ensure it's tidy for the next person to walk in.

A New Habit to follow: Following your evening of watching the television - Remove any items you've used, so that your family room is tidy for the following night.

The New Habit 27, the 27th: Once you wake up in the morning, you should make your bed

The New Habit 28, or 28th day of the week: Following having eaten, throw the dishes in the dishwasher right away rather than waiting.

The New Habit 29, after washing your face, pull out any hairs that aren't in the right direction.

What you might not be aware of is that you are a leader by the example of your family, and these small habits will stick with your after you've practiced for a while and your home will be neat and neat. Do not try to tackle your entire home in one go. De-cluttering can be a great relief but don't tackle the entire house in one go because it makes the job too difficult. If you can establish the habit of a positive one that prevents your home from becoming an unclean place, you can transform your life as well as the overall condition of your house.

Be aware that life isn't a constant thing. If you think of relationships, spirituality, work, home , and the way you conduct yourself as temporary gifts have been handed to you and you will see how changing your perspective on the things you need to complete can go a long way in making your life simpler to manage as well as increasing your chances of success at work as well as your relationships with people. These small adjustments we've suggested throughout the book will be significant once they become regular part of your life. It will be no longer possible to believe that others have done things you ought to have done. You are more comfortable to deal with and your stress level goes down. You feel more energized and happy about who you are.

If you take care of your home by making changes to small habits in your home, you'll notice that less problems in the near future. There won't be the build-up , and you will not have the anxiety of dealing with that build-up since you're taking action now rather than waiting until the situation becomes urgent.

I've put off the final change in habits up to the end of the book, but you can notice the difference these changes to your habits make for your home.

Children are taught to take their toys out when they're done. If you follow this same practice you'll notice that your life is less chaotic. How do you handle all the chores? Cleansing your clothes straight after a meal , or at the very least taking the dishwasher out and washing the counters take minutes. Cleaning up after food has been put out all night can be an absolute nightmare.

How about setting your breakfast table after having had dinner? This is another change in your routine and one that can work for you since it makes you less tasks to complete in the early morning. There are many modifications to your routine that will help you live your life more easily. Cleaning your shoes after you get them off at night ensures that they don't become soiled with dirt. Drying wet towels in the bathroom can create the bathroom smell. But If you are a regular to dry them off on the towel rail it will not.

There is no need to make major changes in your lifestyle for your life to be improved. If you approach things in small steps the world will be changing and it's much easier than you imagine. Make sure that the family and children to modify their routines too and you're on to winning! At the end of this book, you'll understand why I chose to leave the most effective habit to last however for now review your list of routines and consider which habits you can graft onto that concern about the way you and your family lives within the home you are called home. Making changes to your habits will transform everything, without needing to exert any effort or effort at all.

Cleaning up your bathroom after using can save hours of labor after the dirt has gotten stuck to the glass of the shower stall or on the bathtub. You can make your life simpler by creating positive ones that your family members will be able to follow. Include these tiny items and you will improve your own life as well as the lives of the people living in your home significantly easier on a daily every day. If someone is forgetful to remind them, do it in a friendly manner. Make changing your routine a pleasant experience instead of a chore, and you'll win over people whose habits change could be a part of yours to ease the burden.

Chapter 9: Activating The Neurons

We've explained at the start of the book that the neuron groups interact with one another and that infants have more active neurons than adults. Through limiting the activities we engage in, it is possible to shut off certain types of neurons and that's the reason for the adult brains having lower levels of. The conclusion you can draw by this research is that we should to change your habits to alter this pattern. Therefore, for non-creative individuals, changing some of the habits that promote creativity will help their lives. Let's examine the various things that can be altered just by changing the way you think.

Sociability

Spirituality

Creativity

Learning to speak

Relaxation

Anger Management

Discovering new techniques

Control of emotional reactions

Cognitive skills are growing

What you must do is discover who your identity is and also what believe lacks within your own life. As an example, John X was a client who was looking to improve his life. He was never a person who did nothing but work, but he soon realized that due to this, his relationships were struggling while his marital status was in danger. He was unaware that he had the answers within his control. The man was quick to put the blame at other people. The areas in his life he focused on were socialization, relaxation as well as family skills. He also changed his attitude towards work. He started to implement small changes to his habits and it was a huge payoff in time. He was not only capable of relating to others in a more positive way as well, but he was in a position to view the value of work in what it is. It doesn't have to be the sole motive in the life of a person. In fact it was when he managed to implement habits that helped his life become more easy to lead and enjoy, he was amazed that tiny changes could mean many.

Others have reported that small changes to their lifestyles that are healthy has helped them overcome their weight problems, but these weren't mental bending changes. These were simple habits that resulted in losing weight and getting more active. However, others have learned to not be as dependent. If you're emotionally dependent typically, it means you aren't confident in yourself and you do not love yourself enough to feel complete. Nobody else is able to hold your life in order. If you are feeling like you depend on others to shape you into an entire person The type of behavior that you must adopt are ones that help you love yourself to ensure that your contribution to your world becomes more full and less dependent.

It is possible to improve your self-esteem by ensuring that your lifestyle aligns to your own personal philosophy. Therefore, people who found ways to improve their lives could think differently and this is all due to the neurons and the activation of areas of neurons which haven't been utilized for many years. The change in habits can increase the intensity and helps you find something that makes you feel happy. Laura had a tendency to was convinced that her life was going through and she wasn't so happy. Laura was known for telling "yes" to anyone needing assistance. She didn't realize the fact that she was slowly becoming a victim to others. Through introducing behaviors that build her self-confidence She realized that she wasn't able to just declare "no" and "no" but also recognized that it was unhelpful to let the negative people influence what her life would be like.

In this world, you have to be the person you are however, the diversity of humanity lets you dive into areas you've never imagined before and discover an immense sense of fulfillment in your life through changing your routine. You are a worthy human being, and if you do not see worth to your existence, then you have to alter the fundamental aspects of your life you don't like and start to develop habits that will change your life and help you live a more fulfilling life. It's as simple as that. The method of piggybacking your new habits on the old ones or stacking them lets you do it quite quickly and without any thought. If you brush your teeth each day then what's stopping you from getting into the habit of always placing the lid on your toothpaste? If you wake up from the bed every day and you're up for it, what's stopping you from making use of that moment to explore the beautiful day to come and open your curtains and taking note of the changing seasons? All of us have the ability of changing and can trigger those neurons with the changes we make on our own lives. See the optimism at the face of the child. It is not conditioned. It doesn't have preconceptions, and the child's mind indicates an open mind to every possibilities that are available in his/her life. It's the way in which life is lived that snuffs out these possibilities. It's time to regain control of your destiny. The last thing I'll mention that I've mentioned in the book is a beneficial one you could implement after one of your regular routine habits, and that's:

Chapter 10: Breaking Bad Habits From The

Wurzels

Habits form when we are taught ways to resolve some issues. In simple terms that, bad and good habits are created to make it easier to manage the process by utilizing behaviour. There is a reason behind every behavior you participate in. Every habit has its origins typically in response to events that occurred during your lifetime. Everyone reacts differently, even when faced with the same circumstances. One person might react to stress by sleeping, whereas others might choose to drinking alcohol. This indicates that different behaviors may stem from the same source. This chapter will help you'll learn how to recognize the causes of bad habits and figure out what you can do to change the problem. It is founded on the concept that tackling the root causes that lead to bad behaviors is similar to finding bugs on the computer system and solving the cause. If you aren't able to identify the issue fully and correctly, it could cause more issues later. Also, confronting negative habits without taking care to address the root cause can increase the likelihood that the behavior will continue to occur.

Troubleshooting the causes of bad Habits

It is essential to have bad habits discovered first to be able to identify the cause. Each behavior has its own underlying motivations that fuel the surface desire. For instance, you may take a bite of meat because you feel an appetite for food, however the primary motivation is to live. The same is true for eating meat there are reasons behind every practice, no matter if it is either good or not. It is much simpler to determine the root causes that are responsible for good behavior than bad ones. This section is devoted to helping you identify the root cause behind the habits you're trying to understand.

Ask Your Partner

A person who knows you personally is your spouse or your wife. Although they may not be aware of everything, and just as you aren't aware of the root reasons behind your own behavior and habits, their perspective could be helpful. Couples typically spend many hours together, and therefore they are aware of the most about one another. In turn, they may know the exact time when the bad behavior became obvious. They could remind you of the circumstance you were in at the time that the habit began. Your spouse might know the person that they were in love with. If the habit was present prior to the time you were married, your spouse is able to easily inform you of it. If it's something you embraced after the marriage ceremony, then your partner could as well inform you. The analysis of these timeframes aids in narrowing your search and make it easier to determine the reason behind the undesirable behavior.

There are a variety of reasons why your partner is ideal person to determine the root of your bad behavior for you. They are the most effective ways to tell you the reasons behind your habits that aren't working. Your spouse is aware of the ideal moment to inform you of the reasons behind your bad behavior.

Utilize Self-Awareness

It is possible to identify the cause of your habits of bad behavior by yourself. This is possible because of self-awareness. This helps to recognize the start and the patterns of bad routines. A few self-awareness-based practices to consider include journaling and meditation.

Journaling

It involves note-taking of your thoughts and thoughts on your daily actions. So, you'll have an account of what you do each day, regardless of how simple it may appear. A record of your daily routine can help you track each moment of your day. Through reviewing your journal entries you will notice some of your habits are repeated. This can help you become more conscious of your current behavior that you have.

Journaling can help you contemplate the feelings that keep coming back to discover what is driving them. What is it that you are looking for? What was your experience with the craving? What was your response to the desire? It is also possible to identify factors that trigger the craving in relation to time. This can help you identify the root of your habitual behavior.

Development of Habits

The process of eliminating bad habits can be made simpler by knowing how these habits came into being at the beginning. Habits form in different ways and at different times. Different environments can cause people to develop different habits. One of the theories that explain the development of habit is known as one that is called the 3R method. This theory is further discussed in this section.

• Reminders: It is common to keep being reminded to do something because of another evident and well-known behavior. For instance, you may shut off the lights at night as you're getting ready to fall asleep. A reminder is something that causes you to initiate the habit. Simply put, the prompt serves as the trigger to begin the actual habit.

* Routine: The routine now represents the actual act of doing according to the signals

provided in the form of a reminder. This is the process you'll repeat over and over again until it becomes known as the habit.

"Reward": This outlines the reward you'll receive upon having completed the exercise. If the reward you receive is positive the signals will prompt you want to repeat the exercise. Rewarding yourself makes the repeat process more likely, leading to development of the habit. The habit could be irresistible when the reward appeals to you.

Strategies for dealing with bad habits

Knowing how habits are created can help you get in a better place with regards to how you can alter those bad behaviors. Below are some suggestions to provide you with knowledge on how to address the root cause for your negative habits. Note that these tips aren't exhaustive.

Find the cues

You must be able to recognize the signs that lead your behavior the way you're doing. You must examine your behavior and observe factors like the times you engage in your behavior as well as the location, and your feelings. This information will allow you in taking the right methods to break your habit.

Reflect on the reasons for Change

In order to break those bad habits it is important to be aware of the motivations behind changing your habits and concentrate on the reason. In the ideal scenario, the advantages of changing your habits should outweigh the disadvantages of maintaining the old habit. You'll be motivated to stay focused on the new habit. Therefore, you will have an outline of the benefits of getting rid of the habit. Put your list in an appropriate location that you are able to easily access it, so that you're constantly kept in mind of the benefits. This will help you work towards building the habit of a lifetime.

Find a Better Way to Follow

It is possible to change your habit of bad behavior by changing it to a better one. Change the trigger that triggered your previous habit with a different one. If an setting was the trigger behind your bad habits, changing that environment can change the way you do it.

Chapter 11: Slowly But Surely Is Better

Procrastination is a major obstacle to a change in habit. It is imperative to take action for success. If you're looking to transform your bad habits into positive ones, start today. Don't be concerned about how long it'll take. A slower pace of progress is preferable to simply not moving at all. The most important thing is the improvement and the outcomes. The next chapter we'll examine the process of putting more effort in changing your behavior.

According to a new study which was conducted by Phillipa Lally and her colleagues It takes an average of 66 consecutive days to develop an habit (UCL 2009). Following this time you start to implement the routine subconsciously. Be aware that this is a typical period, and some habits may even take longer to develop. The most important thing is the efforts you're putting into to change the behavior. Spend as much time as you can, so long as you're making sure you are not breaking the link that will lead to the end. Below is the method that you can try to establish a routine.

Planning

Make sure you have enough time to consider how you intend to alter your habits. This will assist you in create a plan that you follow through the process of developing an entirely new routine. You can make a schedule that will allow you to set aside time for engaging in the behavior closely related to the habit you'd like to develop. You can also determine the frequency you engage in the behavior over one day, week month, year according to the type of habit you'd like to build. The process of planning helps you get the clear idea of the goals you wish to achieve in order to stay on the right the right track.

Implement Your Plans into Action

Planning isn't difficult, but the real work lies when you put your plans into practice. If you'd like to successfully transform your lifestyle into better ones, then you have to implement the plans you have made. It could not be a single-day thing but your consistent effort will eventually lead you to the goal of success. Be consistent in what you do is the most important thing.

The process of changing a habit is based on repetition of the same process. This is the most important aspect. It's the number of times you perform the same behaviour that is important rather than the amount of time which have passed.

Motion Versus Action

Motion is a lateral motion. It could take place anywhere, including those that are not related to your goal. Motion can be any type of movement even without generating any outcomes. However actions are linked with the generation of outcomes. Planning is a crucial element of altering habits, but it is not able to generate results by itself. It is essential to follow through with your plans. A lot of people do not achieve their goals because they are too so focused on movement. They get distracted by non-productive motion, and lose focus on the action.

Fear is among the primary reasons that people remain in motion for an extended period of time. This might be due to anxiety about those around them. Do you ever feel like you have to do something due to the opinions of others? If so, it also happens when you change your routines. Get your attention off of the people around you and remain glued to your goal of shifting routines. Sometimes, you may be scared to fail. It's an element of learning; simply focus on not to give up. Making a calendar of your activities will help you rid yourself of anxiety. This could cause you to act since the timetable acts as a reminder to follow the behaviors that match your goals for changing behavior.

Common Characteristics of "Non-Quitters"

Habit change is not for people who are not willing to quit, as there are many challenges and highs that are involved throughout the process. In this article we discuss the traits you will find common among people who are not quitters in any field. To be able to make positive changes in your behavior you must be familiar with these characteristics that are as follows:

* Never think of "no" as a possibility It is important to always be aware of your own thoughts. Do not be discouraged by negative comments of others who are around you. However difficult to change your behavior is, you must keep moving forward and remind yourself that you are able to do it. Don't let others choose on your behalf. So, with every "no" you get use it as a way to your success. If you do make a mistake Don't pour all your effort into it. Instead, seek a solution to the issue and continue in the direction of establishing a new way of life.

* Don't expect just to bounce, but also to bounce higher: Don't stop because you have failed. A loss should give you the motivation to move forward. Make sure you have everything you need to ensure that, when you begin new, nothing will hinder you from establishing your own behavior.

* Look at the benefits of success: Failing is typically an element of success. When you're finding it difficult to make changes to

your routine It's part of the process. Keep your eyes on the ball and remember that what lies behind your difficulties and failures is the new habit that you have successfully reinforced.

* Look for setups in each setback: Don't think about obstacles because they serve to help your. Obstacles allow you to become better at tackling issues. Therefore, the temptations you face when trying to alter your behavior can help you build an unbreakable, strong habit.

* Learn from your the fear of failure: It's normal to be scared when you are transitioning from the routine of doing to something which may be completely unfamiliar to you. Although you may not be conscious of what's to come Do not allow the fear to hinder you, but instead to help you learn. It can make you stronger and more focused.

Chapter 12: The Law Of The Least Effort

The chapter will focus specifically on the Law of Least Effort. This chapter will provide a detailed explanation of how it impacts the behavior of humans. We will look at environments that are more conducive to human behavior and strategies for doing things better. We will also explore ways to minimize the friction associated with positive behavior, to help foster and sustain them.

The Principle of Least effort

The concept of the minimum effort was first proposed in the work of French philosopher Guillaume Ferre in 1894. The idea was later accepted and became popular in 1994 under the title "The Law of the Least Effort," when Deepak Chopra published in 1994 a book titled The Seven Spiritual Laws of Success. The law says that it's not worth it to argue about issues that you cannot alter. Also, it suggests that it is unproductive to be worried over the future. In the end, it is better to embrace the events of your life as they are the way you're supposed to take.

Human nature is to choose the simplest method to do things. When you look at all of the inventions people think of they're all in the form of people constantly seeking the easiest solution. For instance, they used to communicate with signals like smoke or drum beats. In the past, people wrote letters, and then the letter would be delivered to its intended recipient following long and tiring journeys. But when the phone was invented, the fashion as well as the speed of communication changed to a entirely different matter. Communication has now become a seamless method of transferring information. Nowadays, people can communicate effortlessly with the help of various platforms like Skype, Whatsapp, Facebook and Zoom.

It is possible to change certain things However, you cannot change every single thing. There is no doubt that with things you can change it is possible to keep investigating and improving your approach to living as the days go by. On the other hand, when it comes to things you can't change it is best to accept responsibility, acceptance and submit.

Acceptance

The beginning stage that is the first stage of the Law of the Least Effort is accepting. Every day, life brings new challenges. As an example, for instance, you might lose your job or might be in a relationship break-up. Instead of being stressed and trying to find what you've lost, the most effective method to manage these situations is to accept the situation as it is. In accordance with the Law of Least Effort, accepting difficult and stressful circumstances can result in improvement. Fight back, or denying the situation can drain more energy from your part, but it will not be successful.

Accepting the reality of a situation can aid you in dealing through it positively. There's a popular phrase that suggests making lemonade from lemons. It goes on to say, "If life gives you lemons, you can use the lemons in the making of lemonade." Louise Hay, one of the contributors to Kidadl's article, said: Kidadl report, went on to state, "If the lemons are damaged, you should remove their seeds, and then plant them to produce fresh lemons (Kidadl Team 2021)". Whatever your current circumstance and practices are, there's always an opportunity to make things better. You may lose your job, but it will further increase your desire to create your own company. Many companies started out in this manner.

Mark Cuban got fired in the 1980s for working as a salesperson in a computer store. This incident provided an opportunity to create his own company, MicroSolutions. From then onwards, Mark has been able to generate more than $2.4 billion (Giang and Horowitz 2013,). Oprah Winfrey wasn't dismissed, but she was relegated from being a reporter to becoming the host of a daytime TV show. The sadness she felt over the loss of her job was not long-lasting, since the talk show was soon a success. She was a highly successful talk-show host. Oprah was one of the most well-known self-made billionaires from the 20th century. Her demotion provided more opportunities to earn money.

Responsibilities

It is important to remember that the Law of Least Effort is not meant to hinder you individuals from being inspired. It is, however, a way to encourage you to be accountable. Responsible people are characterized by their reliability by keeping promises, and observing their commitments. If you're a responsible person, then you will be in control of your life and will not be a victim of excuses when something goes wrong. Being accountable isn't just about self-interest however, it is equally about being compassionate and taking into consideration your surroundings when you make a decision. One of the ways you can demonstrate responsibility are by being honest, performing your job on time and admitting to your mistakes. They will come, but with perseverance they can strengthen you. Therefore, it is crucial to plan your future in a responsible manner.

Submission

Let go of the desire to control everything is among the strategies that can be used to achieve getting in line in accordance with your Law of Least effort. Give everything up and let nature run its course. Overly demanding will result in the loss of energy, and a heightened tension and stress.

Focusing Your Thoughts and the Environment

Priming is an involuntary process where your memory recognizes objects, vocals or specific situations. It can be explained as an reaction to specific stimulus. This method can be utilized to enhance thought processes and patterns using the application of brain functions. Simply put, the process of priming is the process of making preparations or preparing for something. Your mental and behavioral reaction times are enhanced through priming. Priming also helps lower anxiety, stress and depression. Priming can also be used to aid in your studies.

If you train yourself to focus on the negative aspect of things you will see the opposite. However, you should train yourself to see positivity and you will be able to see positive things. So, it's important to set yourself up for positive behaviors so that they be a natural part of your life. To break bad habits you must prepare yourself to be energetic and healthy, by focusing on your exercises. Other techniques that you can use to overcome undesirable habits include hypnotherapy yoga, and meditation. Furthermore the practice of deep breathing and joining support groups for behavioral change are helpful. Believe that you are able to change your unhealthy habit of smoking and you'll succeed in doing so.

The process of priming the environment is to prepare all things that are outside of your own body, in anticipation of an task. Priming the environment is the result of different types of stimuli that are emitted from your environment. Some examples of these stimuli include sounds, taste, images of words, smell or physical movements. You could be ready to be hungry simply by smelling the delicious food you have prepared. If you are looking to work out after work, simply put your outfit in a place where it is easy to see on your way home. It will be simpler to remember what to be doing and easily change into your outfit and get moving.

Different types of priming

There are a variety of priming. This includes the masked, repeated and the negative as well as positive types of priming. Other kinds are semantic and associative priming. These kinds of priming have a variety of uses , and all could be utilized to create desired results.

Priming in negative and positive ways Positive priming increases the time to feedback for the triggered reaction, while negative priming decreases it.

• Repetition-based priming When the brain is exposed to certain types of stimuli and responses the speed of processing will increase in the event that the same trigger occurs. Thus the brain's processing speed will increase.

* Masked priming The stimulus is hidden in a certain way however the brain will detect it and trigger a response.

* Associative priming is typically used when two items or words are connected. Like, for example the cat and mouse. The mere

mention of one could make the brain imagine the other.

* Semantic priming: It refers to words that are logically and linguistically connected. This is illustrated by linking yellow with bananas. Additionally, the sky could be linked to the blue hue.

Good and Bad habits

Like we said earlier, the habits can be a part of your life due to the frequency with which you do certain things. It is essential to build good habits and reduce bad ones. To help promote healthy habits, it is important to lessen the friction that could hinder them, thus making it easier to keep the habit. It is crucial to make it harder for people to break negative habits, so that it is difficult to change them.

Friction in Habits

Every now and then you'll come across resolutions that you make that are based on your determination. While you may be successful in implementing them, most of the time , it's an actual battle. Instead of your willpower the use of your brain could be just what you need to accomplish. Habits, no matter how good or not are stored within your brain. A majority of your everyday actions happen without thinking about it because they are an automatic routine. There is no need to think about them- more as if you're operating doing them automatically. The process of instilling positive habits in your subconscious through techniques like hypnotherapy can encourage the right behaviour. To keep good practices and to stop undesirable ones, it's crucial to regulate your surrounding environment so that it is conducive to the desired changes.

If you create a space that encourages good conduct, you're more likely to stop engaging in bad behavior. For instance, if you aren't looking to eat too much, make sure that you have prepared just the right amount to eat your meals. If you make too much, you might be tempted to eat more because food is readily accessible. If your food is not prepared, you might not want to go through the process again and reduce the risk of eating too much. It is important to note that you must determine the factors that lead to your unhealthy behavior. When you have done that you'll be better positioned to take on them.

Chapter 13: The Procrastination Rule, And

The Two-Minute Rule

The chapter will focus on procrastination. The chapter will address the pain that comes with procrastination, as opposed to the actual pain of working. We will also discuss the two-minute rule more in depth as well as decisive moments. the techniques to study them are all further explained within this section.

Procrastination

The study found the fact that 95% the population within the United States are affected by procrastination (MacKay 2018). If you put off or defer an activity you need to accomplish, it's known as procrastination. If you realize that your curtains require to be cleaned, yet you continue to delay the completion work. A few weeks or more could be passed while the project is hanging. This is a sign of procrastination.

Doing nothing will cost you opportunities. If you see an advertisement that needs someone who is fluent in French. French language. If you've been putting off getting started with your French classes, you'll surely miss out on this opportunity. While you may have the required qualifications, your chances of securing this job are low. You stand a good chance of being denied opportunities if you delay tasks you must complete.

A majority of the decisions you make today can influence your future. It is therefore crucial to focus your thinking and actions to result in great outcomes in the near future. There is an ongoing battle with the past and the future when it comes to implementing good practices. If they are practiced within the current moment, the right practices will bring you to a bright future. If you do not manage to complete the required duties in the present your future might be grim.

There's some discomfort caused by procrastination. Though procrastination could be as a result of laziness, or the discomfort of completing a particular task, the discomfort of delaying the task could be more. When you realize that you've got a job to complete and that task is running through your thoughts and disturbs your peace. The nagging thoughts will continue to haunt you until you take correct step. Once you start doing the work your chances of finishing it will increase. It will be apparent that the discomfort due to procrastination is much more than the actual pain of accomplishing the task. When you are done, you'll feel as if a weight was lifted off your shoulders.

Different types of procrastination

Procrastination is classified in two categories that are chronic and acute. The reason for acute procrastination is typically because of mood or energy changes. It may be triggered by changes in the mind caused by external factors , like having an uninteresting day. Procrastination that is chronically triggered has the more powerful and persistent psychological causes that are difficult to resolve. Let's examine the different kinds of procrastination we can identify.

Procrastination that is acute

Procrastination can be a problem for you. If you feel tired or weak it is possible to exhibit the symptoms of acute procrastination. It is possible to procrastinate when you believe that another person should do the job that was delegated to you. Procrastination can also be a problem at work because of the presence of those you do not like.

In order to tackle this kind of procrastination it is important to understand the motives for your actions. This will allow you pinpoint the exact reason for your procrastination. It is also possible to force yourself to start working with methods such as the timeboxing method. With this method, you plan a specific time for when you will complete specific tasks. Timeboxing lets you decide the time, place and even the length of time you'll be able to devote to a particular task.

It is also possible to improve your energy levels to combat an acute tendency to procrastinate. Do lots of work during the days when you are at your most productive. Afterward, you should take some time to rest and recharge. If the energy level is low go for a walk or take an afternoon nap. When you have resolved the energy problems, you can try to work on the project you've been put off by. If you're emotionally unstable speaking to others can help. Another method to deal with fatigue is to focus on tasks that are easier, rather than.

Procrastination that is chronic

Procrastination that is chronically triggered is more difficult than procrastination that is acute. Stress, self-sabotage and a lack of self-confidence are among the main causes of persistent procrastination. Other reasons include lazyness, unrealistic expectations, unhealthy habits or lack of experience and various cognitive distortions.

To overcome the habit of procrastination that has been a problem for you it is possible to enroll in assertiveness training, take part in groups, or seek out coaches or mentors to assist you. Other suggestions for overcoming persistent procrastination is to overcome anxiety with methods such as visualization, meditation and affirmations.

It is also essential to make sure you don't have unreasonable objectives. Enhance you energy by enhancing your life by exercising as well as getting enough rest and drinking enough fluids and eating a healthy and balanced diet. It is also possible to acquire new abilities that can help you become more productive. Applications for managing time and tasks like Toggl and Trello might be helpful for you. Procrastination that is chronic can be addressed through emotional accounting. Emotional accounting is a method that allows you to talk to your own inner critic, aiding you in promoting or end certain habits.

The Two-Minute Rule

The rule of two minutes was suggested through David Allen, an author of a book titled 2021:"Getting Things Done. The rule says that "If something takes no more than 2 minutes must be completed at the time it's determined" (Allen 2021). If, in other words, the task will take no more than 2 minutes for completion, you could do it quickly and be done with it. Even though the task might be difficult, it's essential to arrange it so that the beginning portion is straightforward and easy to complete. This ensures that you're compelled to get started. Beginning is the toughest aspect, and often causes people to delay their tasks. Once the task has been started the toughest aspect of the task will have been completed.

Have you noticed that when you begin a task and you are inspired to finish it? I have. Think about a situation where someone is beginning their college education. While it can be challenging and exhausting to complete all those assignments and preparing for various tests You will be striving to complete your degree. You'll have conquered the "starting portion" and it's easier to continue to work until the very end. In other words, it would've been useless to begin in the first place.

Benefits of the Two Minute Rule

The rule of two minutes is helpful in many ways. It lets you begin an activity that will eventually become a routine. It is essential to begin the process as it helps you establish the habit. Once you've started with the task, you stand a greater chances of accomplishing the job in a timely and effective manner. The reason is that the amount of focus which initially grows and decreases over time, which will increase the amount of time spent on the job.

The two-minute rule permits you to break big goals into smaller goals. Smaller goals, often referred to as mini-goals can be accomplished. If you do mini-goals frequently, they become part of your routine. If your mini-goals are successful and you can achieve them, it will help build healthy habits.

* It helps you establish a habit. While it might seem like a small step but it is actually simpler to accomplish more. It is crucial to remember that even though good habits can be difficult to maintain however, the key aspect is starting. Once you've begun working on it, it will become simpler.

The two-minute rule helps build the image you'd like to keep. You could go to the fitness center for 10 minutes every day for the duration of a week. While the time spent at the gym may be short but the outcomes from that "short" time will increase with time because of the regularity.

Learning from Experience

If you're looking to kick off with a particular habit then you look into ways to get started. But, it's important not to invest excessive time doing research. Use the knowledge you have acquired to begin an exercise routine that can assist you in achieving your objective. Learn how shed weight is one thing, but actually losing it can be two distinct things. Every now and then, implement the knowledge you've acquired. The more you practice it and the more likely you are of sustaining a certain routine.

The decisive Moment

The moment that is decisive is that moment when you choose to take action that can shape your future. It is at this point that you are able to choose to go for the stairs or spend some moment watching YouTube videos. The decisive moments can affect the efficiency that you have throughout the day. The likelihood of having an productive or unproductive day will be determined by the actions you take during your crucial moments. When you take action on the decision you made to do, your next actions are not conscious. Decisive moments help you develop good habits.

Tips for Making your most important moments count

What you do during your most crucial moments can either create or break a habit. If you choose to take action and then perform it, you'll in a state of mind that you are not paying attention to the task at hand. It will become an automatic process and shape your future. Therefore, it's essential to be aware of what to do when that crucial moment arrives. Here are some helpful strategies that you can use.

Make a plan ahead of time: Based on your objectives you can develop an annual, weekly or daily schedule of the things you'd like to accomplish, based on their importance. Choose the most important items on your list, and then begin doing the ones you want to do.

Be aware and thoughtful If you're calculating and aware, you are able to complete tasks which are more productive and beneficial to you. In general, more productive work will lead to the development of healthy habits.

Stop the waiting Make it a routine to move quickly following critical instances. There's a well-known phrase that says, "Success favors speed." By grabbing the moment, it can help you complete the task with the determination, allowing you to build the habits you want to and become more efficient.

* Reward yourself: After completing certain tasks, reward yourself. This will encourage you to work harder by encouraging the habits you want to develop and ensuring you are productive.

• Create a feedback process Keep track of your weekly, daily or monthly tasks and assess their effectiveness. This will allow you to determine what is working and allows you to enhance your work execution for the next time.

You should think about finding a partner to share the experience with: Finding a person with whom you can carry out the same activity might well be a way to establish a habit. If, for instance, you do not want to miss working out and want to invite a buddy so that you can exercise together. This way, it'll be very difficult to skip the workout since you're the person who made the invitation.

* Learn to get to understand yourself It is crucial to know your own self and find out when you typically experience most crucial moments. In the case of some people, this may be the first thing in the morning. When you get up you might get that decisive moment that can get your through each day. It is essential to understand your schedule so that you can follow through and establish healthy routines.

Chapter 14: The Study Of Good And Bad

Habits

The chapter will be focused on the study of bad and good behaviors. We will examine ways in which healthy habits can be developed. We will also go more deeply into changing behavior, and the six stages of change in behavior. In this chapter are some tips on creating good habits.

Good Habits

Good habits are the actions that lead to positive changesand encourage your personal and professional development. The goal can be achieved when you have positive habits. Research has revealed that, apart of goals, people feel motivated by behavior. It is possible to be motivated to adopt positive habits through reflection about your progress towards your objectives.

How to Develop Good Habits

There are many methods to develop healthy practices. You can determine what you would like to achieve by writing down your personal and professional goals down in writing. Each goal you can create an action plan for how you'll get there. Develop good habits to ensure you can incorporate them into your life. For instance, you could establish a routine to dress for the next day, the night prior to. It is essential to review your routine to assess your progress and adjust if needed.

In order to establish a positive habit creating self-discipline is crucial. An artifact, treasure map or a visual representation of your goals will help you to build self-control and establish good habits. To develop good habits, it may require you to have support from your family, colleagues, and your friends. You can also use apps like Stickk(r) to receive assistance in trying to establish positive habits. The app allows users to enter an objective and get an instructor who will assess the progress you make as you progress.

Bad Habits

Bad habits are a bad behavior pattern. These bad habits could include lying or jealousy, to smoking, eating unhealthy or drinking, excessive use of mobile smartphones, playing games, cutting the nose of your child, as well as many more. While you might intentionally or unintentionally engage in a harmful behavior, you won't be satisfied with the results. It is therefore crucial to focus your attention on changing your behavior in a way that gradually gets rid of undesirable behaviors.

Behavior Change

Change in behavior involves the breaking of an existing habit and a shift to new, and often controversial methods of living. Simple things like going for a run in the morning can take longer than anticipated before it is a habit. It is important to think through and deal with your shortcomings or any issues in order to create an effective program for behavioral change. When you're trying to make a change in your behavior it is essential to realize that changing your habits isn't an easy task. It is best to take small steps at a time and allow yourself enough time to adapt. Changes in behavior can be classified in six steps. These must be recognized to help smooth the process.

The Six Steps of the Behavioral Change

Six stages of change resulted from an investigation on the cessation of smoking (Cherry 2019, 2019b). These are the stages smokers who participated in the study went through. These stages generally apply to any person who is taking on this challenge to alter their their habits.

"Street One," the initial stage is called the pre-contemplation. This stage is distinguished by a lack of concern for the need to change. In this stage one is not aware of the need to make changes. The stage is marked by assertions like, "Does their behavior change actually affect their life?" Let's take the example of losing weight. One can eat whatever they want, without taking the impact of their diet on their health.

Stage Two: At this stage, the person isn't sure what they desire to achieve. They think about changing and consider the advantages and drawbacks to making the new lifestyle. You may even imagine yourself as the body they want to be at this point.

* Stage Three: The person is preparing to make changing their lifestyle. They are planning to help assist in facilitating a change of behavior. One example is that one could enroll in sessions on behavioral change. Additionally, one could be looking into ways to eat healthier.

The fourth stage is Stage 4. At this stage the strategies are put in action. People begin to practice the habits they plan to establish. In this stage, they begin going to the classes they took up. They begin monitoring their diet and exercise routine as well.

"Stage Five": The behavior is kept and becomes a routine. The person will be accustomed to healthy food choices and exercise is a part of their daily routine.

"The last stage is known as the relapse stage. This is the time when a person reverts back to their previous habits. Their old habits deteriorate and ends in this stage. A person is hooked by unhealthy food and indulge in binge eating, as well as other bad eating habits.

There are times when you be in several of these phases. It is crucial to remember that changing your habits isn't simple. You must be patient to be able to navigate the change with ease. Recognize the changes you make along the way. Don't be rigid and cruel to yourself. Make sure you learn by observing your own mistakes, and remain on the right track.

The Commitment "Device"

An instrument of commitment is present decision made by an individual that determines the future actions. It forces you to act in a specific manner in the future, by sticking to your good habits and shielding your body from the bad habits. If you are trying to prevent eating too much, you should purchase less food as well as cook less. If you suffer from an addiction to gambling You can request to be blacklisted on casinos and online poker sites. This will keep you from playing if you are feeling the urge to.

The tools for preventing commitments prevent you from being lured into engaging in enticements by changing the tasks so that it is more demanding to follow the bad thing than perform the beneficial one. The likelihood of doing the right choice in the future is raised by first making it harder to commit to an unwise habit. Are you looking forward to the community fun run that is coming on? Contact the organizers and inform them that you'd like to be a part of. Once you've done that, the excuses to not attend is embarrassing, so don't try the same thing again.

Additional Tips for Making Positive Habits a Reality

Technology makes it easy to establish good habits that are a necessity. Some actions may not be as regular as they might be become routines. Certain activities may need to be done on a monthly or even on a yearly basis. These could be things like the payment of tuition fees, rent payments and even payments for insurance bills. Transferring these to the expert knowledge of technology doesn't only mean you successful in implementing an excellent habit however, you also avoid the wrong one.

A variety of suggestions are available to help make positive habits a reality. They can be categorized as intrinsic or external aspects. Here are some suggestions you can apply to build good habits.

Find Your 'Why'

It is crucial to understand the reasons behind why you would like to start the right habit. If you are trying to change your behavior to please others it is possible to find yourself disappointed. At first you may feel excited. With time you will lose interest and stop doing the routine. You may even relapse but if you continue to act to please other people It is more likely you'll experience disappointment again since motivation comes from outside. This cycle can continue until you discover your "why. Knowing the reasons you're looking to alter your behaviour will make you more excited. If your enthusiasm comes coming from your own inner self it is possible to successfully implement any behavior.

Connect with people who are like you

Being around like-minded people is a way to be sure that you will see a shift in your behaviors. Have you ever noticed when your closest friends or family members are engaged in a habit you'd like to quit It becomes very difficult to end it? I've experienced this myself. Imagine a situation where you're determined to eat well and your partner is always eating fast food often delivered to your home. So, it becomes more difficult to eat a balanced diet.

Take it slow

As was mentioned previously it isn't easy. When you are trying to change a habit, you need to take it step-by-step to achieve success. If you attempt to do everything in one go, you will encounter difficulties. But, if you break down your fitness goals into smaller goals that can be accomplished each day, small steps can be counted as success over the long term. For instance, an hour of walking every day will yield positive results if you consistently follow. This is distinct from attending the gym, and performing exercises until exhausted to the point of having to take an entire week off due to the exhaustion. As per James Clear, it is advised to establish the following small-scale habits that can be easily managed.

Change Your Lifestyle It's not about your life.

A complete overhaul of your lifestyle can be difficult. Sure, you might have big goals but it is best to concentrate on small changes which will result in the achievement of your goals in the long run. Small routines that can be repeated over and over will help make your big goals become reality. Lifting your legs to lose 50 pounds is life-changing . However, performing them three times a week is now a way of life. Do you realize the difference between these two? The latter will yield more results than the former.

In addition to the previously mentioned guidelines, there's also an invention known as the Pavlok. It's a gadget you wear in your hand, and it helps in the eradication of bad habits and encouragement of healthy ones. The device produces electrical stimuli and vibrating sounds that help make your brain more tolerant of bad habits and to develop an appreciation for good ones.

Chapter 15: The Habit Loop

The three phases of a habit are called phases, referred to as"the "habit loop." The initial phase of the loop known as"the "cue" also known as"trigger" or "trigger." It's an event that your brain has over time created a particular response. The response, of course is what we refer to as an habit (Chen and. al., 2020).

Psychologists have observed that almost every habit is triggered by the context. There are two kinds of cues from the environment that psychologists refer to as "direct cueing" and "motivational cueing." Direct cueing is the process of establishing relationships between certain routines and specific settings (Chen and. al., 2020). For instance, if you're always reading in the same place or sitting in the same chair at night you'll be compelled to read every time you go into that space. It might be difficult to concentrate or to study elsewhere However, the association between the reading space and that particular room instantly prepares your brain to focus and be focused.

Motivational cueing, on other hand, is based on rewarding. If you drink coffee in the morning and it can make you feel more alert and alert, you're most likely to consume it again in the following day. If giving your partner flowers makes her feel happy and you're sure to purchase flowers for her to celebrate the holiday that comes around. Positive results from actions (or that don't immediately yield negative outcomes) will more often develop into habits since we're more likely to repeat them.

All behaviors, whether either good or bad can be triggered by a type of signal (Chen and. al., 2020). Your brain is able to tell that it's time to start the habit. Consider your actions as mental programming. Your brain is programmed to respond to certain signals. When your brain detects signals, it activates the correct program. To develop new habits or change previous ones, you must understand what your signals are since they're not always clear. It's possible to think that you drink your coffee in the morning since it makes you feel awake So you substitute coffee with water, green tea and natural energy supplements, food that is carb-based... but nothing. Then you quit, concluding that there's no way to alter the coffee habit. Perhaps the caffeine isn't the cause of your coffee consumption at all. What happens if you placed the coffee maker in a different location of your home? Do you have to go all the way to the basement or go into the living area to search for your coffee? Maybe your cue isn't really motivating after all and is more clear. The reason isn't caffeine, but the smell of your kitchen at the beginning of the hours of the morning.

In reality, there's plenty of evidence to suggest that when a behavior is an habit, triggers from the environment can be more effective in comparison to promises for an incentive. This is why it's difficult to break habits even when they no longer reward. It's because the reward, also known as motivational trigger, might be the reason that initially prompted you to begin the habit, but once it becomes a habit the trigger that initiates the loop within your brain is nearly always a result of environmental (Chen and co. 2020).

For instance, when driving your car, do your consider placing your foot down on the brake when you come across an red light? Do you do it in a way that is automatic? When you first began beginning to learn to drive it was likely that you had to take a conscious decision to step on the brake. However, now all you need to do is to see an red light or stop signal for the routine cycle of slowing down to begin. When you first started learning the habit, the motivation for you was rewards (not the possibility of crashing your vehicle). As the habit is ingrained and the trigger has nothing to do with hitting the car. It's now an automatic reaction to an external stimulus (the green light).

It's a lot of "red lights" everywhere which trigger automatic responses that are not our knowledge. It's possible that you'll start feeling hungry around noon, due to hunger or you hear music emanating out of the truck from which you normally buy lunch. The habit of eating lunch isn't driven due to a need that is inherent for food, it's triggered instead by the sound your brain has come to associate as food. This is why sleep experts generally recommend not doing anything other than sleeping in bed. When your room is solely to be used for sleeping, then your brain will begin to associate sleeping to being in bed. Just the act of sitting down will cause you to get exhausted. If you do not watch television, read, or browse through your phone and eat dinner in the bed, your brain will not make a connection between sleep and bed. It could even form an association between sleep and other activities. As soon as you fall asleep and your brain isn't trying to get ready for sleep, it could get excited and eager to watch TV or check out social media.

A study in 2012 proved the effectiveness of contextual triggers to trigger automatic responses to habit (Wood 2017). The study separated participants into those who were habitual in running on a daily basis and those who were only occasional runners and those who did not exercise at all. The first step was to list their favorite places they ran (or would normally run for non-runners).

Researchers asked participants to imagine the location they chose as their usual running spot. They then requested participants to read a brief piece of text and highlight their names "running" as well as "jogging" each time they were mentioned on the page. The study revealed that regular runners were more able to locate the words than those who ran sporadic or not. However, the study also revealed they were unable to identify these words significantly decreased in the absence of being instructed to imagine their normal places to run in the prior to doing so. The study revealed that just picturing their running route could make runners more apt to run until they became more sensitive to the phrase "running." It was found that the location and activity trigger similar responses to the brain. People who had not yet formed the habit of running On the other hand were not yet forming the associative connections to their running routes.

The Routine

Imagine the routine as a habit that it is. This is the behaviour that happens automatically whenever we're exposed to a specific environmental trigger. If you've done enough, you'll be immediately prompted to think and behave in a specific way in similar situations, without any particular purpose or expectation of outcomes. This is the reason you reduce your voice whenever you visit a library, or begin to think about distant relatives in the days after Halloween. Your brain automatically associates library with the dropping of your voice. It also connects Thanksgiving with calling distant relatives. The events are an opportunity to press the "play" button for the behavior, attitude or emotions that you've associated with the situation.

If you begin being aware of your personal habits, you can begin to observe the entire process from beginning to finish. If you are tempted to smoke smoking cigarettes or thinking about the chocolate you're supposed to be having Pay attention to the surroundings around you. What triggers the craving? Was it the location? Who are you with? What time of the day? Are you heading to someplace? Did you just return home from another location? The better you get in recognizing the signs of your environment that you are aware of, the more aware become of your personal habit loops.

On the other hand you could also utilize the effect of context clues to build your personal habit loops. If you are a habit of doing your homework at the library, you'll realize that walking towards the library puts you into the attitude to do your research. If you're a habit of timing your exercise to coincide with sunrise, you could be able to see an early dawn light, or even the chirp of birds at certain times in the morning can make you feel feeling energized and ready to go out. The routine may be in the middle of the routine loop but it's also the part of the loop where has the least amount to control. The more closely the action is to some specific signal that cue, the more automatic it is (Chen and others. 2020).

The more times you do, think or even say something in a specific setting, the easier it becomes to think, do or say something when you next find yourself in that particular environment. The more automatic an action becomes, the more relaxed it is. For instance, talking loudly in a church for instance, is likely to be something you'll have to think about doing as it could seem odd or incongruous. Even if the venue was not crowded It would be uncomfortable to be loud because this kind of behavior will be in opposition to your normal of a loop. You've formed a connection between church and whispers, and therefore, any other behavior will make you be very uncomfortable.

Routine activities are in the neural networks of our. In time, the brain develops certain connections when we are exposed to external or environmental signals. Repetition is what forms this network of pathways. It requires repeated repetition in order to build new ones. When you begin to behave in a manner that is in opposition to your usual routine the brain is in an unknown territory. When you change your surroundings or altering your behavior within a familiar space you're making your brain make new connections. This is the reason why beginning the process of creating a new habit or ending the old one can be difficult at first regardless of whether it's advantageous or gives you an incentive. It's not enough to get an excellent night's sleep or a day that feels rejuvenated and refreshed. You must repeat the same behaviour over and over again and establish new associations with your environment until it becomes at ease.

Psychologists are able to classify every human action into two categories: habitual and goal-directed (Chen and co. 2020). Goal-directed behaviors are the conscious choices we make every day. They are the methods by how we react to the new situation and new information. They are heavily influenced by the consequences. If confronted with any new circumstance we naturally choose the path that we believe will be most likely to serve us at the time.

But the habitual behaviors are reflexive. They are done not in anticipation of a particular outcome instead, as a reaction to a trigger situational. While most habits start as goal-oriented behaviors and become more routine, the more automatic they develop and the less influence that the outcome will have over how the behavior is carried out. This is the reason you find yourself eating that extra piece of cake or staying up one more hour even knowing it's not good for your health. That's why you're not able to avoid going out with your friends , even when you must get up earlier the next day and you are tempted to put off work when your favorite friend calls you. If you're used to the routine of having a chat with your favorite acquaintance every afternoon, the benefits of picking up or not answering aren't much of an impact on the decision to take the call. Naturally, you'd like to speak to your friend however, your phone is in your ear before even having thought about that thought. The most difficult part of trying to break or create the habit, however, is underestimating the strength and impact of rewards in the loop of habit.

Not surprisingly, the more simple an activity easier to perform, the faster it can become a habit. A study conducted in 2010 revealed that it took just 18 days of repeating basic tasks such as riding a bike as well as drinking more water, to get habitual however, it took on average 254 days of continuous repetition before things such as exercising become routine (Duhigg 2014). The reason behind this is that it is more to do with the environment, rather than the rewards. Simple or "recurrent" tasks can be done in the exact same method, regardless of the changing conditions in the environment. Drinking water while hiking or in a class and at work is almost identical, particularly when you have water bottles with you. The ability to repeat drinking water all day long is incredibly impressive.

On the other hand complicated and "nonrecurrent" tasks require adjustments in order to be executed, based on the external environment. When you're trying to build the habit of visiting the gym each day after work All it takes is one day of being required to stay up late or being invited out with colleagues to alter your ability to complete the same task. The more that your ability to perform the task affected more time it takes for the behavior to become routine. The issue isn't how strongly you'd like to hit the fitness center. As long as your brain doesn't form sufficient contextual connections that you'll need to constantly remind yourself to hit the fitness center.

The Reward

A reward can be described as the most important element in the loop of habit and , as such, is a distinct piece of the loop. Once a behavior is a habit, reward will have little impact on the extent to which we do the behavior. However, to have a behavior repeated enough to be an habit initially there must be some sort of reward. At a minimum the action must assist us in avoiding some sort penalty or adverse consequence.

Habit loops don't only create themselves around repetition; they develop around satisfying and successful repetition. The satisfaction of completing the task is great and so we repeat it over and over again. As time passes our brains decide that X is the most appropriate response to the situation. Once the behavior is automatic, the brain does not require the promise of reward to perform the behavior any longer. The reward is already assumed. If the incentive is altered or disappears completely the habit is so well-established that, for it to be overtaken, it has to be replaced with a new behavior that is rewarded with a new reward.

Although identifying the cue is an essential aspect of habit formation, knowing the reward is just as vital. It is possible that the trigger and reward are two different sides of the one coin. Imagine, for instance, that the habit you're trying to stop is that you are biting your nails. Whatever you do but you are unable to stop. You've covered your fingernails with lemon juice, put on gloves, and even started painting your nails but in vain. However, the main problem with every one of these strategies is that they fail to tackle the motivation behind it that led you to start the habit at all in the first place. It's likely that you didn't begin chewing your nails to taste delicious or because you love how your nails look after you've eaten them. To end this habit, you need to look at your own feet and determine the loop of habit that it's a part of. What was the reason you started to bite your nails in the beginning? What is the motivation that led you to keep repeating the same behavior?

For many people, nail biting can be a response to stress. Stress-related feelings are the trigger or trigger, while stress relief is the reward, therefore your routine will appear as follows: stressnail-biting -and stress relief. In this moment it is possible that nail-biting will not be able to relieve anxiety, but the habit is now automatic. If you want to end or change your behaviour, you must to change it to a different behaviour that gives you the same rewards. The use of gloves and dip your fingers in lemon juice most likely, are not the best stress relieving methods. If you're in stressful situations , or you feel the need for biting nails try doing something that helps you relax. Replace your nail-biting habit with meditation or a deep breathing exercise. Establish the habit loop of your choice one that triggers positive behavior in stressful situations and that will provide the purpose of easing anxiety.

The rewards we receive (or have received) from routine behaviors aren't always apparent. Socializing, satisfaction, distraction as well as self-punishment and even pure joy are all possible rewards when we've completed our daily loops. In a manner or the other, we've got our behaviors start as coping strategies methods that we've developed to handle certain situations in our favor. Once you've identified the external factors that lead to your regular behaviors, the next thing to consider is whether the behavior itself has made it easier to navigate the environment. For instance, maybe you're always feeling the need to smoke cigarettes when stressed. How does smoking cigarettes relieve anxiety? Do you think it is merely a way to distract yourself and something else to consider in times of anxiety? Perhaps you have gotten into the habit of discussing the stress with your friends while in the park smoking cigarettes. After a while you're in a new place and your buddies have gone away however, the act of smoking cigarettes is now an element of a routine that used to bring the satisfaction of social interaction. The way you choose to behave to replace smoking will be effective if it builds an equivalent bridge between the surroundings and the rewards.

The achievement of a specific reward is usually the trigger that initiates the creation of new routines. When we're consciously seeking to master new behaviors However, the goals and the rewards that we receive at the conclusion of our routine loops may not always coincide. For instance, if are trying to establish the routine of eating well-balanced foods then the reward you're trying to obtain is likely to be something to improve your mental or physical wellness. However, the benefits you reap from eating unhealthy food aren't likely be a part of your new diet plan. In addition, the benefits you reap by eating junk food may not be as you believe they are. It is possible that you begun eating junk food simply because it's tasty and you've begun eating junk food at the lowest point of your life. Perhaps foods like ice cream , mac and cheese or hamburgers helped you feel better because they remind you of summer picnics, childhood memories or other occasions in your life where you felt loved and happy. The pleasure of having junk foods, in the end it has less to do with the taste, but more with security. Your new diet will not bring this reward as you don't have the same feelings. To really change your food habits that are unhealthy then you'll need discover new ways of living that will yield the same rewards in similar circumstances.

If we consider a particular habit to be "bad," it's typically due to the fact that there's a reason why the behavior can be detrimental to our lives. However, even "bad" practices can be rewarding in a variety of ways. Shopping for pleasure may cause you to feel guilty because it drains your savings as well as clutters your house and can make you feel guilty about spending money in a way that isn't necessary. However, chances are it's still fulfilling the desire it was designed to attain which is sufficient to feel secure as well as comforting. Knowing the signals that prompt you to begin shopping online will usually aid in identifying the rewards that shopping can bring you. When you're next in a similar circumstance Try implementing a new behaviour that will bring the same rewards.

3

Why Willpower isn't Working

W

Habits become automatic when the habits are... they're automatic. Because you don't make conscious decisions to follow them, making a decision not to follow them won't change your behaviour or at the very least, at least not over the long run. The patterns of the neurological brain that are created by habit are evident to researchers. Once the pathways are established, it's not easy to eliminate them. To change behavior that is ingrained the pathways must be altered. Reward and triggers require to be linked by different responses.

Automatism is such a potent aspect of habitual behavior that this is the way scientists differentiate between goal-oriented and habitual behavior. If you can change or stop the behavior due to the fact that you aren't happy with the result or because the outcome did not match what you had hoped for and you are able to see it from an evolutionary perspective the behavior can't be considered to be a habit. Habits are actions that you repeat repeatedly and consistently regardless of the result. The diminishing power of reward that is a part of the habitual behavior is referred to as "outcome sensitivities." Even when the initial reward has been fulfilled or has not been fulfilled by the behaviour, the appropriate triggers will trigger the response that is accustomed to it (Wood 2017,).

But, even though the majority of behavioral psychologists and cognitive scientists acknowledge that willpower alone can't be enough to alter habits There is some debate about the role that willpower (our ability to regulate or regulate our behavior) is in transforming habits. While some argue that willpower doesn't have much to have to do with it, some behavioral psychologists argue that a degree of willpower is needed to inspire you to make a change in your behavior initially. Many have said that the capacity to alter habits is linked to self-esteem. The more self-esteem you have higher your capacity to alter your habits.

The lower self-esteem you have is, the more prone you are to damaging habits.

While these kinds of psychological theories can't be verified through neuroscientific studies However, one thing is for certain that willpower alone does not suffice for two primary reasons (Wood 2017). The first is that trying to fight habits using willpower is a mistake because it underestimates the power of their habitual nature. It doesn't matter how much you'd like to cut your nails or run every day. When you're exposed to the environment's stimuli, you'll be more likely to repeat the same behaviors without even realizing you're doing. The second reason is that willpower can be emotionally draining. Human brains respond more strongly to the lure of instant sensory pleasure than to any other form of stimulation, such as the abstention from punishment or the ability to reach the long-term objectives. Therefore, declaring "no" in front of yourself a few times per day won't be enough to stop your behavior. In time your willpower will wear out and you'll end up back to where you were. This is the reason why changing or changing your habits is more effective than just trying to break them.

Instead of just changing or stopping routines This book is concentrated on changing the way you think about them. To achieve this it requires an amount of willpower. Willpower is the reason you are able to make changes in beginning. Willpower is what will motivate you to change one habit with another. It's what prompts you to look closer at your behavior and help you recognize habits that assist you in making relationships between rewards and cues.

When combined with the appropriate strategy for habit-changing willpower can be an effective source of energy and motivation. Willpower can keep you focused when it comes to moving to transform your life to the best. But it's not the only way to go to transformation. In the case of change in habits, willpower is only effective when coupled with clear objectives and a defined substitution behavior.

When it comes to habit change behavior psychotherapist Mark Manson insists that focusing on willpower is placing too much focus on the final aim. The way to decide if the habits we engage in can be described as "good" as opposed to "bad" is to look at them in relation to larger goals in life. We make the decision that drinking alcohol every night or eating cookies prior to eating dinner is "bad" behaviors since we're trying to shed weight or be healthier. The prospect of losing weight in the near future will not be enough to break the routines have been forming around eating, exercising or another aspect of your daily life that you've identified as getting behind you in getting to your goal. It's the willpower that will give you direction. It helps you identify which habits you need to be changed and at what point. The willpower system is like your GPS, however just plugging in your route doesn't suffice to bring you to your destination. In order to achieve this you must break down your routines into tiny loops. You must determine which circumstances trigger your negative habits, then determine which routines or actions you'd like in their place and then determine how these new routines or habits will bring about the same results that you enjoyed from your previous habits.

From a neurologic perspective Willpower is not a factor in have anything to do with the transformation of habits. Willpower is found in a region of your brain referred to as the prefrontal cortex. This is the area of your brain that controls conscious thinking, problem solving and decision-making. Goal-driven behavior is initiated by your prefrontal cortex. When those behaviors are incorporated into a routine that region of the brain ceases to light up. The pathways that are habitual are created within different areas in the brain. These are regions that regulate how we respond to both environmental or emotional triggers. From a neurological perspective willpower and habits are like apples and lemons. From a psychological perspective willpower is an effective motivational tool. It's the fuel you put in your tank, it's the element that drives you to take on such an intimidating undertaking as redirecting your brain. If you don't have willpower, it's unlikely to progress much in the area of changing your habits. Willpower is just one tiny part in the whole puzzle.

The Research

A research study was conducted to determine how effective the concept of outcome insensitivity really is (Duhigg 2014). In the research, participants were shown a sequence of images. They were told that if they responded with one of the images would get them candy, and the other one would reward them with potato chips. After a couple of hours of repeatedly expressing their preferences when responding to the images, participants were given their choice of snack. They were offered the amount they could consume until they were satisfied. If tested again, participants were able to make almost 100% of the images, despite declaring that they no longer required or desired the food they previously chose. Their responses to the specified images were already automatic regardless of the actual result (Duhigg 2014).).

This study does not only reveal how powerful the effect insensitivity can be, but it also illustrates how fast an easy step can become an habit. The easier the task, and the faster your reward more quickly the pathways to habitualization are created within the brain. This is why motivating you with goals, beliefs or concepts may not be so effective as we would like them to be. For instance, your ambition could be to become an accomplished writer, however, you're spending the majority of your time watching Netflix instead of writing your novel. It doesn't mean you don't possess the qualities is required to be a successful writer. Simply having an idea of what you want to do isn't enough. Being a successful novelist is an amazing objective however there are a myriad of ways to reach this objective. The benefit of writing an outstanding novel is something that can be enjoyed in the long run. Habits however do not respond with the longer term. They are a part of immediate sensations, sensory or the familiar. If you've spent the last couple of months on Netflix from 8pm until 2am each night, at 8pm you'll have a difficult time trying to focus on anything else.

The most ardently desired goals are often characterized by what psychologists refer to as "equifinality." That means they can be accomplished via a variety of methods of behavior. The more choices you have available to you the less likely you will be to create a pattern of behaviour. The goals are vast. They're complex. Most importantly, they're deliberate. Habits however aren't consciously planned. They're automatic. It's the consequence of conditioning not motivation. Changes in motivation could be a result of a change in goals however, it doesn't always indicate a change in behavior.

In reality, there's lots of evidence to suggest that a connection between self-control with performance in the habit may reduce your chances of being able to make significant changes within your own life. If you think that changing your habits is a matter of willpower then you'll consider your performance in the habit as the failure or insecurity. When you are tempted to engage in the old routine you'll see it as a reflection of your motivational skills or self-control. The inevitable feelings of demoralization that follow each repetition of the old routine can eventually prevent you from attempting to change or, even more so, prompt you to take on new actions which are designed as a way to "punish" you. Self-punishing behaviours can result in a much more serious psychological impact than bad habits, and when they are taken to the extreme, could cause physical harm too.

Controlling unwanted habits and behaviours is a subject that humans have studied for long periods of time (Sims 2018). Control of behavior was previously an area reserved for state religions However, in our current time it's becoming more the province of psychologists and scientists. Through the years many different strategies have been developed to assist the common person cope with undesirable behavior thoughts, emotions, or thoughts. However, at the end all, most widespread and effective strategies for self-control are not dependent on desire by itself. In everything from the strength of praying to the twelve-step AA program, all methods for controlling behavior begin with the need to change. However, all effective habit-changing methods or programs provide an approach to change the habit that is undesirable.

A study from 2010 examined the effectiveness of various methods people employ to stop unwanted behavior or emotional urges throughout their entire lives (Wood & Runger, 2016). Around 12% of undesirable impulses that were reported by the participants of the study were classified as "strongly regular," meaning that they were actions that were performed every throughout the day in similar settings. 38percent of unwelcome stimuli were caused by emotional circumstances (Wood and Runger, 2016). The behaviors may not have been practiced regularly however they were carried out automatically in response to specific emotional triggers, such as depression, stress or even sexual arousal. Although all of these actions can be considered to be routines in the sense that they were automatically performed as a response to a specific event, the strategies for coping which worked for routine, incidentally triggers habits did not necessarily work for behaviors that were emotionally triggers or vice versa.

This is the reason understanding habits loops is essential to a successful change in habits. Knowing the trigger and the first reward can make an important difference in the strategy you take to tackle the habit. An habit that is caused by anxiety will not be handled in the same manner like a habit that is triggered by the time of day. In addition, it is important to note that behaviors that trigger emotions are prone to different types of rewards than routine ones that are based on deliberate repetition. Tieing your left shoe first for instance, might be without reward whatsoever. It's because you're left-handed, which means that you chose to tie your shoe on the left shoe the very first time you tied a shoe. However, because nothing transpired to stop you from beginning by tying your left foot, it has never thought of changing the way you tie your shoes. If you decided to alter this habit, the methods that you'd employ are different from the strategies that you'd employ to break your drinking habits on Saturday mornings. It started as a college ritual that you began with your buddies, and was then a regular thing with the event-driven trigger of Saturday mornings as well as the prior reward of time spent with your buddies.

"The Myth of Self-Control

Self-control occurs when we are conscious of the choice to not do something that we actually would like to do. Self-control is the reason you decide to make your mind up to leave the New Year Eve celebration at 11:00 pm because you've got a major task due on January 2nd and you have to get up early the next morning to continue working. Self-control is the way you decide to finish your homework before you sit down to watch television and also how you choose not to drink alcohol when you're in the hospital. Self-control is part of the prefrontal cortex and it has a lot of influence to how we handle different situations or deal with our life's challenges. However, self-control is largely unrelated with the habits we have developed.

Particularly Self-control is more effective at stifling behavior that is caused by everyday situations. If you wish to get to your alarm an hour early for instance you set your alarm for the right time. As it sounds the alarm, your brain is filled with images of the fantastic new job you just received and pull yourself from the bed. Repeat this process a few times and you'll have an entirely new routine. It sounds simple, right?

This sort of thinking isn't working when our habits trigger emotions. The issue is when we aren't sure if our triggers are caused by circumstances (time of day or physical environment, conditions) and emotional (stress or depression, sensual pleasure). If it's normal for you to rise at 7am because it's what you've always done, making yourself wake up at 6am could be feasible.

Imagine that you dislike your job. You are a hater of your boss, you're not able to get along with your coworkers as well as you're certainly underpaid. The snooze button in this case, may be more than just a matter of willpower in the end. You're in the habit of sleeping through the night until 7am, because you don't want get up for work, and not because you're familiar with waking up at 6 am. In this case the trigger that triggers you to press the snooze key isn't triggered by routine. It's caused by anxiety and fear of getting to work.

Imagine that you are offered an exciting new job. You're in love with the job. It's everything you've always wanted. The work environment is excellent and you're comfortable well with colleagues and you're in a field you are enthusiastic about. Yet, you're not able to get up from your bed in time. Why? Because your brain has created an association between your alarm going off and your upcoming job you don't like. Before you realise what you've done, you've clicked the snooze button and fallen back asleep. Willpower can alert you of your habit however in this instance it won't suffice to alter your behavior.

Numerous studies have revealed an effective method is to alter or eliminate the triggers that trigger unwanted habit loops (Wood 2017, 2017). It's much simpler said than done. Habits are often created without intention so it's often difficult to determine which triggers it is, or even what the original reward was. A study from 2010 found that self-monitoring with care was more efficient than avoidance of triggers, due to the fact that a lot of participants didn't know the triggers that triggered them (Manson 2019,). However, the study revealed that this intensive self-monitoring method was just marginally more effective in changing undesirable behaviors.

Self-control (what the study calls "vigilant surveillance") is much better at alerting us to our automatic behaviors and impulses however, it's not a good method of resolving undesirable behaviour. It's almost impossible to alter behavior without a certain amount of self-control. But self-control is only the beginning step (Manson 2019).

Numerous studies have also revealed that self-control is more complex than it appears. Things like the distraction of others, cognitive decline that is related to aging, stress or even a lack of capability to complete tasks can all take away the self-control of an individual. Even if stress isn't the primary cause for your habits and you'll feel less in control of your actions when you're exhausted, distracted or otherwise impaired in your cognitive abilities in comparison to when you're calm and focused. Since it's a given that you won't be at peace and focus 100 all the time and it's likely that a lapse in cognitive capacity will derail your self-control when it comes to regulating or stopping an unwelcome behavior.

The decision to behave differently in a situation that is familiar requires determination. If your willpower resources are exhausted or weakened due to other demands on your brain then you are bound to rely to your routine behaviors to get through the current situation. For example an investigation conducted in 2005 examined participants who had developed the practice of disclosing private thoughts private. Everyone in the study were striving to improve their capacity to share personal thoughts or thoughts (Wood 2017,). When they were relaxed and focused, they showed the ability to modify their usual behaviors. However, when participants were required to complete an uncomplicated task prior to entering a social context and were more likely to revert to their previous habits even when disclosure of personal information was the most appropriate social action. The feeling of fatigue or disorientation caused them to lose their ability to control themselves, and prevented them from making permanent changes to their behavior in social situations.

The best way to make long-lasting, positive change in your behavior is to develop new habits which are neurologically competitive with the existing ones. Self-control is what motivates you to make this change however, it's not enough to change the neural pathways of your brain. The process of transforming your habit is the process of creating automaticity around good behaviours. Instead of consciously seeking to express your emotions for instance, a successful change will require you to find alternatives that provide the same feeling of safety that withdrawal from emotions gave you in social situations. Self-control is usually the factor that helps you be aware of the automatic responses you make. At first, basic self-control could be the factor that helps you understand what your true reward or triggers are. However, the self-control alone will not be enough to change, alter or alter your habits.

4

The importance of a goal

B

Before you can begin exerting your willpower to change your behavior Before you begin making changes, you should set a clear objective in place. The goals will help you understand the reason you're trying to change your behavior at all. In addition, they provide you guidance on what you'd like to do to change your behavior. You'll be able to find yourself with greater motivation when you're aware of the reason you're trying to change your habits and what you're hoping to gain by altering your routines and habits.

To change your behavior it is necessary to have an adequate reason. The reason you want to change your behavior is an internal compass or compass that you can adhere to when things become difficult. Willpower by itself is not enough when it's used out of context. If you're looking to sleep earlier or eat more nutritious food it must be backed by an underlying reason. The uninformed, frequently socially motivated reasons such as "being healthier" are not often good enough to motivate you to stick with it. Why do you need to change your behavior? What is it about your habits that makes them "bad"? What of your goals in life do you have a habit that is preventing you from reaching? What kind of hardships are you creating that could be avoided by changing your habit into something productive?

The realization that our habits have gone bad is usually at a time that Alcoholics Anonymous calls "rock low." This usually is an event in our lives that is significant or a negative and dramatic event which was caused by the bad behavior of the issue. Although it is possible to alter your habits prior to hitting the bottom, most of us do not believe we're in trouble until something drastic occurs. The effects of our habits are often tiny. It's therefore easy to think that they have no large impact on life's quality and that we can change our behaviour at any moment and at any time if we chose to. It's uncomfortable to think of our bodies as living machines that play recordings of our behavior in response to specific environmental triggers. We like to think that we're in complete control of our choices, consequently, we believe we're not doing anything to change our behavior because it "isn't an issue" or that it's not the "real" issue. When we reach the bottom that we are left with no choice but to look at ourselves as the person we are, and acknowledge that there's more that governs our actions than conscious, active making decisions.

Most effective objectives are those that are specific. They answer directly the question "Why should I end or change this habit?" As an example we will look at the case of Lisa (Duhigg 2014). She was plagued by a myriad of problematic, addictive behavior. Her addiction was to drinking and smoking. She was a shrewd spending addict, and had a difficult time controlling her anger and discovered herself with more than $20k in debts from credit cards that were not paid by 30 years old. At the age of 40, she'd completely changed her life. Not only did she manage to stop drinking, smoking and even shopping, she also was a professional with a great career and a good credit score and was in better physical form than when she was just 25. What did she do?

Although it's easy to think that Lisa was simply a victim of the will of a king (and definitely, willpower came into play during her journey) There's much of more that the above. The reason that drove her to make a change in her life was an event that was dramatic. Like many others, had to go to low before she was capable of admitting that her behavior was destructive and beyond her control. Her bottom was reached as a result of the divorce of her husband. Following that, the couple and their new partner took off for Cairo. Lisa was with them and was thinking of taking revenge on her husband who had left her. After a tense confrontation that her husband declared that they were never going to get back together and she decided to go on an excursion across to the Egyptian desert. She was unsure if the trip was feasible however one thing was for certain: to be able to take the trip, she'd need to stop smoking.

Lisa's decision not to smoke was directly tied to the accomplishment of a certain goal, which was to make the journey over the desert. This was the "why," this goal which prompted her to give up smoking and switch to the more healthy exercise of jogging. Although it could seem like a stretch to think to quit smoking and help her completely transform the corner, changing one habit caused an unintended effect throughout her life. In the end, several of the factors that triggered her other vices were directly related to the triggers which drove that she smoked. Actually, certain practices (like drinking) are caused by smoking tobacco! Although bigger, more vague objectives like becoming healthier are definitely worthwhile but they're not the best incentive for changing habits due to the fact that they're too large and vague. However, the tiny, specific purpose of traveling over the Egyptian desert was just right, and it was enough for

Lisa to not just stop smoking, but also change her lifestyle completely.

Habits are tiny specific actions that can only be triggered by specific situations. They do not respond well to huge goals that are long-term in nature since it's so easy to integrate a behavior into vague, large-scale plans. It's possible that you're determined to quit smoking to "live more healthily," but it's too easy to reach that objective by eating a healthy diet or taking a yoga class every morning. In addition, getting "healthy" doesn't mean you'll get a tangible benefit, something you're able to work towards and surely attain. This does not mean that it's not an important target, but as long it comes to habits it's not concrete enough to inspire motivation to make changes. The goal Lisa set, in contrast was small and precise. It was an incentive for her to quit smoking and the prospect of the trip provided enough motivation to keep changing her habits even when the process was hard. It was a predetermined schedule, so that there was no way for her to fall back into old habits. Every single day she smoked a cigarette instead of taking an exercise routine, she was denying herself the dream of taking her journey back.

Chapter 16: Setting Goals

When you set goals, it's crucial to stay true to your goals and not just what you believe is feasible. Since most of our actions are not noticed, we have an instinct to set goals based on our behavior. To be successful in achieving the lifestyles that we would like to live it is necessary to adopt an opposite approach. Setting realistic goals allows you to develop habits that are based on your objectives.

In many instances the loss of willpower in changing habits is often associated with a shift in your subconscious objectives. If you consume alcohol, or go at the bar on weekends, the more difficult it is to imagine yourself pursuing your dreams of becoming surgeon. As time goes by you begin to convince yourself that surgery "isn't suitable for people like you" which means your capability to control your unhealthy habits is ever more restricted because your goals seem less and more impossible to achieve.

This is the reason why the act of writing your goals down is so effective. Instead of allowing your habitual behavior to dictate the things it is that you "can" or "can't" do by writing down your goals, it provides you with a tangible reminder of the goals you'd like to accomplish. It will also remind you that you are able to achieve your target, and that changing your behavior is just the first step of your long-term strategy. Focusing at the ultimate goal that you truly want will give you the drive you require to change even the most deeply-rooted habits.

In addition, setting goals can help you identify the best way to alter your routine. For instance, if your aim is to become excellent writer, you may be able to replace your drinking with writing or with open mic night. If you want to become surgeon, you may prefer replacing your drinking with exercise, or you could replace your parties with studies. Set goals that are specific will allow you determine which behaviors can be considered "bad" to begin with in the beginning. Anything that is hindering you from getting your goals is something that needs to be changed to something that gets the goal closer, or maintain your lifestyle you desire (Wood 2017).

If you're not aware of their habit loops are left to think of the causes that led them to develop a routine. If you're aware of the behaviour however, you're not aware of the trigger and the reason, you'll are able to think about what caused the behavior at all. Most people are prone to believe that if an action is frequent and difficult to get rid of, it must coincide in some way with the "true" desires or needs. Studies have revealed that individuals believe that their the behavior is beneficial because of how difficult alternatives are. For instance, one study of consumer behavior showed that consumers tend to stay making use of the same products or services due to routine (Dean 2013,). However, when asked why they were hesitant to trying new skills or products the majority of participants claimed they believed that brand new (unfamiliar) product was somehow less effective. An examination that was objective of the two goods or services showed that this was not the case. This study proved how difficult it is to see habitual behaviors as the reasons they're based on, and also how easy it can be to make assumptions about our or others, as well as the world that surrounds us based on what is at ease. Everyone thinks they're immune to this type thought, however how many times have you thought something like "Well I suppose if I truly wanted to be a member of the band, it won't be as difficult to learn on my instrument" or "I definitely need to take this test However, it's equally important to me to build strong relationships with my peers. It's possible to skip this particular night ..."

This rationalizations minimize the effectiveness of habits. Indeed, numerous studies in psychology have demonstrated that the existence of bad habits has nothing to do with be related to the ability to establish strong goals or objectives. We all know that the promises of reward or the desire to achieve a specific outcome has no influence on behavior that has developed into a routine. Habits can be persistent and difficult to break just because they're automatic. If a behavior is especially challenging to overcome, it isn't necessarily a sign of some sort of internal conflict, or provide any insight into the motivation behind you to reach your goals. Do not set goals based upon your behavior. Change your habits to help you attain your objectives (Duhigg 2014).

Sometimes, the compulsions or habitual behaviors are so intense that people create internal motivations to explain their inability to alter (Wood 2017). The majority of addicts complain about their compulsive urge to drink or take substances. But some studies have indicated that this urge is not the cause of using drugs or alcohol, but rather an excuse for the behavior after the actual. Similar things happen in those who suffer from obsessive compulsive behaviours. The habitual behavior is not a result of any type of conscious decision being taken. To better know what we're about and why we do this We can look back and determine what was going through our heads when we were engaged in our habitual behaviour. The risk is that it could lead us to reach specific conclusions as to who really are and the amount of influence we have on our lives.

Goals can assist you in avoiding the same conclusions. Your goals have more to tell you about your character goals, aspirations, and inner motives than your behavior. Instead of letting your obsessive actions define who you are instead, look towards your goals and let your determination to achieve your goals be the primary factor that defines your personality. Goal setting is a way for us see habits as what they really are: automated programs that used to serve us but have stopped working as they should. Setting goals will allow you to not only identify the patterns that need to be changed, but also be aware of the loops they're a part of. Understanding the signals and rewards will allow you select the best substitute routines that can not only transform your habit but also bring you closer to your own personal goals and goals.

The power of Intention

If our habits are based on our intentions We find that switching between one habit and another much simpler. Imagine, for instance, that you've made the decision to change from eating white bread to whole-grain bread. You purchase it from the grocery store for several weeks. You discover that you enjoy it, especially when you use specific spreads or butters, and therefore you buy it. After a while you're seeking out whole grain bread white bread becomes gone. This is where habit transformation can benefit you. When you set your goal to eat healthier and you identify the habits that hinder your goal You then choose a new habit that aligns with your goal when you are exposed by the exact triggers and you continue until the new habit has surpassed the previous one.

The use of intention as a tool to change your habits isn't just limited to physical actions either. The emotional and mental habits are greatly benefited by intention-setting and intention setting. Perhaps, for instance, you've started to feel resentful towards your partner because they're selfish. A friend from the same circle says you're being too harsh and supplies numerous examples of instances where your partner was generous and selfless. You decide to make an effort to appreciate selfless behavior from your partner. You keep a note each time they purchase you drinks or come over to listen to your concerns. Then, before you know it the habit of describing your partner as selfish has changed.

Intentions serve as a guidance to our behavior. They tell us what we'd like to change and the ways we can make them change. The reason is because intentions help us to see patterns and our brains are awestruck by patterns. As a species, we have a great ability at recognizing patterns. We are wired to appreciate repetition, to a certain extent and that love of repetition can be utilized to rapidly and quickly change bad habits into productive ones, if we set the intention of guiding us.

A good example of how effective pattern recognition is in our brains can be found in an old psychological study. Participants were seated in front of personal computers for a total duration of around four hours. They were required to press one of four buttons in accordance with the location which location the image of the cross appeared upon their screen. The only thing they were not informed is that there existed a specific pattern in how the cross appeared on screen. The pattern was not consciously discernible at first, but throughout over four hours they were able to react quicker and faster to cross's movements in the display. Through repetition in blind, participants learned the pattern without even noticing they had a pattern to be learned.

This is how the patterns are created within our brains. We are confronted with the same scenario repeatedly, and then respond in the way that is most beneficial our needs at that moment. If we get similar rewards by repeating the same action a number of times, the behavior becomes a routine. We've developed the pattern, that is, the pattern loop and not even realizing. It's usually only when the pattern breaks and the loop doesn't reward us but actually causes us to suffer and harm, that we realize the existence of the pattern at all.

With intent, however we take the conscious decision to study (and to unlearn) the specific behavior or mental model. Unconscious patterns can create any kind of behavior and thoughts in our minds. Setting goals and intentions is the best way to avoid these random patterns and assists us develop habits that are beneficial for us. Through intention, we are able to build an array of tiny habits that will help us reach more difficult objectives. Consider learning complicated mathematics or the language of another country. At first it's incredibly difficult. You'll spend hours scouring flash cards trying to remember "red" means "roja" and "hello" means "hola." After repeated practice, new words phrases, words, and grammar become easier and more easily. Once you've become accustomed to these patterns and a habit, you're able to begin to master more complicated phrases and words.

Habit transformation is the most effective when we set huge life goals to identify the behaviors we wish to instil into our minds and which needs to be rewritten in favour of something completely new. As with learning a new language Goals can assist you develop positive habits that are built on each other. If your main goal in life would be to "be rich," for example, setting your intention will aid in breaking the goal into smaller everyday actions that will allow you to reach your goal and keep it up when you've achieved it. Starting beginning with "hello" as well as "goodbye," your initial goals will be basic and simple such as "save $5 per each week" and "make the coffee in your home, instead of purchasing it at Starbucks." When these routines have become habitual and a part of your routine, you can begin to build upon these, eventually creating an intricate network of positive practices that are all working together to help you reach your goal of living a life wealthy.

The intentions of our minds usually feed directly into our routines. When we are in the mood for something, we seek ways to obtain it. The desire for something is so strong and essential that numerous psychological studies have shown intentions are the top one predictor of behavior in the future. If you are consciously deciding that you'd like to become wealthy and you're more likely to save more than someone who does not. But, it's essential to be able to think regarding our goals because if we don'tdo so, our brains will search for patterns in the first place. A lot of our behaviors (especially those that aren't good ones) are completely accidental. We are in a specific place or in the presence of certain people and then, all of a sudden we're surrounded by all these behavior patterns that do not have anything in common with our purposes or motives. Actually, these behavior patterns could be in opposition to our ideals and our inventions. If we're not aware of this it's easy to conclude that these powerful routine behaviors were crafted to serve a purpose, and that the emergence of the habit is related to have to do with the things we "truly" would like or what we really are.

If you are setting your own goals Don't be afraid or embarrassed to establish goals that are true to you. For instance, if you're trying to quit smoking cigarettes, but the idea is "being healthy" does not seem to motivate you, consider reasons to stop smoking that reflect your lifestyle. Perhaps a more compelling motive could be to provide an environment that is healthy for your kids, or because cigarettes can be expensive and you'd like in order to reduce your expenses. Don't let the society dictate your choices for you. Stay true to yourself and committed to your objectives. Your habits will be much easier to change once they begin to be in line with what you truly desire for yourself rather than the things you believe you ought to want for yourself.

5

Making Changes to Your Habits

H

Abit loops cannot be eliminated. When your brain has built neuronal connections they cannot be removed. They are, however, able to be replaced. Imagine your neural pathways as wires. They aren't going to be discarded and begin from scratch however, you can shift them around and create new connections. Quitting for good isn't enough. To stop a bad habit you need to pick an alternative or something that is more beneficial to replace the old behavior.

This section will give you a the practical steps to change your habits. It doesn't matter how deep-rooted your habit is, or what you want to change that habit, the approach is able to help you. Although this process is easy but it's not always straightforward. The process of changing habits isn't easy. It takes time for the new behavior to feel relaxed and natural. If you're struggling with an addiction to drugs it is possible that you will experience negative physical results. If the behavior you want to change is the potential to trigger emotions, you might need to test a number of alternative behaviors until you can find one that gives the same level of emotional satisfaction. However, remember that you are able to do it. The key to habit formation is repetition. If you persist with it, you'll be able change regardless of how difficult it may seem initially.

Before you create a clear goal or begin the three-step process but first, you must determine the trigger. What emotional or environmental trigger creates the habit loop you're trying to end? The process of determining the cause may be a lengthy process, particularly with habits that have been going for a long time. Take your time during the process. Be aware of the environment and your mental state when you notice yourself engaged in the undesirable behaviour. What triggers the loop? Was it the "play" key that led your brain to start the program? It could be something simple however it could be something else. A lot of habits are born out of a desire to do so However, many habits happen in the course of accidental events. Things that trigger your actions could be a surprise to you. It could be that they appear as if they are not connected with the act or reward. The things that trigger negative behavior are those that we're not willing to acknowledge are able to influence our lives. However, identifying the trigger is essential to a effective change in habits. If you don't understand what's creating the habit loop you'll end up engaging in the behavior , without being able to understand the reason. The trigger can help you determine the actual advantages you've previously derived from the behaviour, and it will assist you in find the most suitable alternative behaviour.

There is no have to join an expensive formal treatment program to get rid of a bad habit regardless of how severe or damaging it may be. People can change their lives by themselves constantly. It's not always simple however it is certainly doable. The hardest aspect is the honest self-reflection that is needed at the beginning to begin the journey. To change your behavior completely you'll need take a hard examination of the signals or cravings that motivate and trigger your undesirable behaviors and figure out ways to replace destructive habits by positive ones.

The most significant aspect of habit modification The most important aspect of habit change is, however, this final step. Without a new routine permanent change is virtually impossible. These old habits won't disappear from your mind, regardless of how powerful your resolve is, or how hard you attempt to stay clear of the triggers of the past. It's impossible to alter the way your brain functions and you aren't able to control the environment around you. Whatever your resolve want to "quit," you'll inevitably be exposed to old signals, regardless of whether these cues come from feelings of boredom or stress or even environmental signals like being in a specific area. Once your brain has received the signal and responds, it'll engage in the same old behaviour. It is the only method to end this cycle is to provide your brain a different response, or a different game that responds to the similar signal.

The studies of alcohol-related alcoholics have shown that those who experience lasting change are those who discover new routines that use the triggers from their previous ones and also provide the same level of relief (Wood 2017). In analyzing their routines and their triggers, they realized that they were unable to alter the triggers and that their brains would continue to crave the pleasures that alcohol used to provide. To stop completely drinking, they'd need to replace their drinking habits by one that could be incorporated in the previous habit loop. If you decide to change your lifestyle The goal isn't to end or eliminate your habits. It's about removing your middle-of-the-road routine, and replace it with something more useful, something that can also provide a reward in response to the trigger in the environment and aid you in creating the lifestyle that's in line with your goals for the long term.

Even if you're not participating in a treatment plan that is formal However, it doesn't suggest that you should fight your addiction on your own. Indeed, numerous studies have proven that your odds of success transformation are much higher when you work as in a group (Wood 2017, 2017). Believe that you can accomplish it is essential. If you lose hope or think that your old ways are invincible You'll lose the motivation to keep your commitment. A membership in an organization or community will allow you to keep faith in yourself and believe in your the possibility of success. Communities offer support when you're struggling and also examples of other people who have fought successfully the same struggles you're facing right now. If you can try to find other individuals or groups you can use to help you break your behavior. Find another person be it a family member or a colleague, or a community on the internet, that is suffering from similar habits. However bizarre or unique your habits are most likely that there's another person out there who is struggling with the same issue. They might have different triggers or be getting different rewards If you can discover someone who can transform together, there's the benefit of emotional support of having someone who is cheering your efforts.

The 3-Step Process

This easy, three-step procedure is a way to discover yourself. These steps will assist you identify the habit loops that you are prone to. You'll become aware of your triggers as well as your reward, which will allow you to select the appropriate and beneficial substitute behaviour. Recognizing habit loops can be more complicated than it appears as such, so following these steps might take time and thought. Be mindful of your own. For many doing these things generally takes longer than actually changing their behavior!

Step One is Awareness Training

The first step to changing your behavior is to watch your behavior. This is when you'll be able to be able to recognize your triggers and the rewards. If you're able to keep a diary, you'll record your thoughts and begin to look for patterns. Keep your eyes on the events around you as you begin to develop the habit. When you begin to bite on your nail, can your fingers feel an itchy or tingling sensation on your fingernails? Are you feeling anxious or worried? Are you with a particular person or at a certain location? What is the exact time of day? What time of the year? Are there any specific holidays approaching? Are you heading home after an occasion? Try to be as aware as you can of the surroundings. Note every aspect of your surroundings as well as internally each time you see yourself engaged in the unproductive behaviour. In time, you'll begin to observe patterns. These patterns will assist you identify your cues.

Take your time during this process, since it could take some time to think about. Perhaps, for instance, you're trying to change the habit of purchasing a coffee when you go to work. It's likely that your workspace or office is your environmental indicator but is there something that's happening? You are more likely want your morning cup of coffee when in a stressful state or when the commute is especially difficult? Are there any particular social or personal situation you think you're missing out by not buying you don't buy that coffee? If you prepare your coffee at home prior to going into work buy a cup of coffee once you arrive at work? Do you want coffee around the same time each morning on weekends, or even when you're away on vacation? It could be due to the fact that you're at work or home, but it's not always the case. Particularly, the benefits that you receive from your cup of coffee might not be what you would like to see. If coffee is how you get your brain going every morning, making your own coffee at home could suffice to reduce your desire. However, it's not enough to prevent your brain from playing with that program once you go to work. If you want to keep yourself from purchasing that cup of coffee, you'll need to come up with a new routine, or something else to do before you start work. It will be satisfying exactly the same way.

Second Step: What is the reason why do You Do This?

After you've identified the trigger then the second step would be to decide the reward. This is often more challenging than determining what's your trigger. Therefore, you must be patient with yourself. The rewards we reap from our regular behavior aren't always evident. If this is something that you've had for years it's possible that the initial rewards not apply anymore or could be irrelevant to the current circumstances. However, determining the reward is an essential step, so you must be mindful while you search for the solution. The reward will help you determine what kind of routine replacement are most suitable. A major hurdles to a successful change in habits is when people attempt to change their routines with new ones that are appropriate for their situation but don't satisfy with the satisfaction the old routines were satisfying. In order to make a lasting change, you need to come up with a new, effective method to earn yourself the same benefits. To accomplish this it is necessary to identify what the rewards will be.

Rewards needn't be tangible, however. A lot of habits are created unintentionally to satisfy fundamental needs like anxiety relief and distraction from boredom the desire to connect with others or feelings of hunger. Boredom and stress particularly are two mental states that can be very mentally demanding. Certain habits are developed to aid our brains deal with these stressful mental states. The actions it selects to alleviate these emotions, but they are usually random, and are more likely in common with the surroundings where these habits were formed rather than the mental state of mind itself.

Imagine, for instance, that the behavior you're trying to get rid of is that you go to the cafeteria to grab a bite after only one hour of working. It's a routine: you get to work at 9 am and by 10am, you're in the cafeteria. You think it's because you're hungry early in the early morning. It's possible that you feel a sense of hunger at this point. To stop this habit you've tried bringing nutritious snacks for work, having more of a breakfast, and even eating lunch earlier, but all without success. The reason why none strategy works is that the benefit you receive from visiting the cafeteria isn't the relief you're seeking, but boredom relief. The method you select to replace your breakfast snack, however, should be one that eases the feelings of boredom to be effective instead of satisfying the cravings. If you can find a substitute routine that piques your interest You will likely find that your hunger in the morning disappear.

Sometimes, to discover the real benefits of our bad habits it is necessary to test several different substitutes. In the case of the breakfast meal, you may try to replace your morning walk by eating a healthy meal at your home. However, if it's not working If you're dropping your lunchbox day in and day, then you might decide to look at whether your alternative routine is bringing the same benefits that your destructive behavior.

Step Three The Reward

After you've identified the actual consequences of your destructive actions and you'll have an instant of clarity. "After having my nails bitten I'm feeling emotionally fulfilled." "After having my breakfast coffee , I'm ready and excited to get to get started." "After taking a bite of an entire chocolaty bar I'm feeling that my meal is done." When you discover the source of your destructive behavior selecting the most appropriate replacement behavior is easy and easy, particularly with a clear objective in mind. Understanding the reasons you want to change your behavior and recognizing the it is that your emotional or sensory reward behavior is able to satisfy and can enable you to make the process of changes much simpler and more efficient.

After you've completed the three-step procedure, you'll be able to choose a new routine and take the necessary steps to change your life. There's a chance that the replacement method you've picked doesn't perform, but that's fine. If you're in a good knowledge of the habit loop and its components, both in terms of its cues and reward, you'll be more successful in selecting a substitute habit that you can believe you will be able to commit to. When you choose a routine to replace keep in mind that the less complicated the action, the simpler it will become into an established habit. The most efficient method to change destructive habits is to choose a substitute routine that is less complicated than the destructive one. The more simple it is to master your new routine more easy it will be to replicate it.

This three-step procedure is designed to make you aware of the habit loops you are in. This is the only way to help you develop an action plan you'll actually be willing to follow. Whatever way your new behavior is a part of the old routine be aware that it may initially be uncomfortable. Habits are behaviors that have been repeated over and over time. This means that regardless of how harmful or unpleasant they've become they're also familiar. The brain is wired want to feel familiar. Making a change to something completely different can be thrilling, enjoyable and satisfying however, it could also make you feel uncomfortable. Whichever method you decide to substitute for your previous routine, allow yourself the space to allow it test before you decide to alter or attempt another approach. Initial attempts you try it will always be uncomfortable. It's one of the reasons why it's so difficult to get used to (Duhigg 2014).

If possible you can, consider replacing your destructive habits by doing things that you've always wanted to try but did not possess time or "time" to complete. Consider, for instance, that you've always wanted study a new language. If you're ever tempted to reach for cigarettes or the TV remote opt for your smartphone instead. Utilize the time you'd otherwise take to take "smoke break" or watching television to learn Spanish through a language-learning application.

To illustrate how the three-step procedure can help you develop a successful plan to change your habits We'll take a look at some examples.

Example #1 A: Biting Nails

You're looking to quit biting your nails as it is against your goals of looking attractive or healthy. You may find yourself biting your nails to respond to anxiety or stress or anxiety, and when you engage in the habit you experience a feeling of happiness. If you want to stop this habit, then you can try a routine such as chewing gum or taking deep breaths. These habits will help improve your lifestyle and bring it closer to your objectives of living better health or maintaining more hygiene. Instead of painting your nails or dipping them into lemon juice, these routines have been and have been proven to decrease anxiety and boost the sense of security. Therefore, these alternatives are much simpler to stick to since they provide the same level of relief during times of stress that nail biting used to provide.

Exemple #2: Coffee Addiction

You'd like to quit having coffee in the morning since buying daily cup of coffee is against your financial objectives, and is in contradiction to your dietary goals , as it makes your body addicted to caffeine to awake in the morning. After drinking your coffee you're relaxed and ready for work. Drinking coffee in your house prior to going to work will not fill the gap that your morning coffee isn't satisfying. To replace it you can try drinking tea with herbs or water in place on coffee at the beginning of the week. Even if you buy a tea at the exact place the teas can be less expensive as coffee beverages. Both of these drinks therefore, will help improve your lifestyle closer to your objectives of saving money, and also avoid being dependent on caffeine. They also will allow you to keep your current regimen as much as you can particularly if you buy coffee from the exact store or drink your water from the same mug you previously drank your coffee in.

Example #3: Eating Chocolate After Dinner

You're trying to break your habit of eating chocolate immediately after dinner since it goes against your diet goals of eating less sugar and the goal of losing a specific number of pounds. Whatever the size of your dinner eating chocolate is now a habit for you. Therefore, you won't feel full until you've eaten the chocolate bar. One possible alternative might be to eat an assortment of sweet fruits like strawberries or grapes following dinner. Since sweet fruits do not contain processed sugars, this method can keep your routine in line with your goal of eating lesser sugar, and dropping weight. Separately eating fruit will substitute for the traditional eating of the chocolate, which will help keep you full without consuming more food. Additionally, the fruit's sweetness will make you feel as if you're still eating treats or desserts and makes this routine simpler to stick to rather than substituting the chocolate bar with a salty snack such as potato chips or peanuts.

6

Try out New Routines

A

At at this point you've completed the 3 step process and are now able to pinpoint your loop. As an example, your loop could look like this: boredom - going to the cafeteria for food--distraction. For instance, anxiety--biting your nails--stress relief. Now is the time to come up with a strategy.

In the three components of your loop of habit, only the one thing that is likely to change is the middle, which is the troublesome behavior. The aim is to replace this behaviour with something positive and productive. The trigger will stay the same because it's something you can't reasonably expect yourself to manage. The reward has to remain the same for the new behavior to be effective.

The type of cue as well as the reward you receive will decide which alternative behaviour is the most suitable. In this regard you might need to test a variety of alternatives before you can find one that stays. For instance nail biting is a frequent habit that is usually triggered by stress and anxiety. If you're also experiencing these triggers, you could consider deep breathing or other techniques for mindfulness as a suitable substitute for the habit.

But, as was Mary Sims' case Mary Sims, simple stress reduction methods didn't suffice to end her nail-biting habit (Sims 2018, 2018). Why? because there was another signal that caused her to specifically adopt the habit of stress management of nail-biting. It involved dental fixation. The act of placing something into her mouth was the primary reason for her to have unconsciously established this particular habit instead of developing a different way to reduce stress. The deep breath could provide the same effect and could provide the appropriate in response to the trigger however, it did not meet the oral obsession.

When she realized that, Mary changed her tactic. Instead of trying to substitute her nail-biting by the deep breath, she substituted the habit by chewing gum. This helped to alleviate both anxiety and oral habit that led her to start her habit of. Chewing gum was found in numerous studies to help reduce anxiety (Duhigg 2014) and Mary was not an exception. After years years of trying various strategies to stop her addiction Chewing gum was the best way for her stop the "unbreakable" habit in just a few months.

However, this doesn't mean it wasn't simple. Mary was required to ensure she always had a bag of gum with her throughout the day to ensure that whenever she was stressed she had a chewing gum stick to chew rather than cutting her nails. Repetition is the most important factor to the success of changing habits. If she was feeling overwhelmed and didn't have any gum and she was stressed, she would immediately go back to her old routine to bite her nails. After a couple of months of constant repeated practice, she had realized she didn't have the urge of biting nails. Gradually, but gradually her gum habit replaced her nail biting habit. In addition, she have gorgeous nail, she also had drastically reduced her chance of developing infections, and also had an added benefit of having fresh minty breath (Sims 2018, 2018).

Another instance of a long-term, "hopeless" nail biter is Mandy (Duhigg 2014). When she was just twenty-four, her nail biting habit was getting so severe that she would frequently bite at her nails until they started to bleed. At times she would bit her nails till they fell off from the skin beneath. The fingertips were covered with scabs, her hands had become swollen and distorted with no nails to protect them. She was also beginning to experience tingles and sharp painful pains in her hands which is usually a indication that nerves had been damaged.

Along with compromising your health, her nail biting habit was ruining the social aspect of her life. Mandy was embarrassed by her peers and kept her fingers tucked inside her pockets and was unable to have dates or meet people. She tried every one of the traditional tricks, like painting her nails and submerging her fingers into lemon juice however, to no avail.

But when the counselor at her state college's counseling center requested her to follow the three-step procedure it was possible to determine her pattern of behavior. The trigger, it was discovered was boredom. The reward was not just disorientation, but also an actual sensation from her tooth rubbing her fingers. Therapy suggested new method that would give her the satisfaction of feeling some sort of a physical sensation on her fingertips. She had to test various ways of doing it like the practice of putting her hands into their pockets or knocking at the desk every whenever she felt the desire to bite off her nails. Then, she discovered a method that worked: rub her elbows using her fingertips. It's an amazingly easy solution for a situation which had caused many emotional and physical pain in the life of Mandy. But she wouldn't have find a resolution without first knowing her triggers, and rewarding. She wouldn't be able to come to the solution without trying out other substitute behaviors.

As with Mary like Mary and Mandy You may need to try a variety of alternative behaviors until you discover one that is suitable for you. After you've identified your habitual loop, you could uncover additional layers or nuances to your life when you test different alternatives. The process of experimentation is a an essential part in the learning process. Always be mindful of yourself. Every time you try a new habit will provide more information about yourself. It will provide you with insights into the reasons you started this habitand could even reveal specific details about the events in your daily life when it first started. Find ways to inspire yourself to be committed to your new habits If you are able get other people involved in the process of changing so they can support and encourage you!

Example of a Routine for Addictions

Smoking and snacking are two habitual behaviors that millions of people fight each day. Although there are a myriad of harmful habits that could be destructive that are not harmful, smoking and snorting are frequently considered to be the ones are desirable to end since they're visible and cause a large quantity of damage quickly, and they're difficult to end.

Snacking, whether it's sweets and sweets, salty snacks or even sweet drinks such as soda is frequent occurrence in our modern world due to the unimaginable accessibility to junk food. In the present it's not often that you are in a position that you don't have access to chocolate chips, chips or soda, ice cream or anything else filled with sugar, salt or fat. If you're not in a position to get access to these items, all you need is a quick visit into the grocery store, or a stroll through the neighborhood to the local coffee store to fill your desire.

Snacking is a great way to show the power of the 3-step system because it's a widespread routine that can have unexpected triggers. Many people are unable to manage their snacking habits since they believe that the reason is hungry. This is only logical isn't it? To stop their addiction it is a struggle to substitute the food with healthier options but then find themselves going back to their previous ways after a few weeks.

To stop the habit of snacking, however it isn't necessary to eliminate the snack and the behaviour, but to modify the habits. It is only after following the three-step method that people realize that their habit of snacking might not be curable simply because of hunger. People may have started to snack in order to deal with anxiety, depression or boredom. It could also be used to help them get things done. If your eating habits are aiding in the relief of boredom or even an excuse to get away from a difficult project at work or at home, replacing the food with a salad isn't likely be enough to satisfy. Alternatives include walking for a stroll and allowing yourself five minutes to look through your social media feed or making a 15-minute conversation with your partner while you typically snack are all better alternatives.

Smoking cigarettes is a different practice that's notoriously hard to quit due to the assumption that we are given cues from our culture. Although nicotine is an physical addiction however, the triggers that led to the development of the habit initially aren't necessarily linked to nicotine itself. The majority of the time, nicotine addiction and the habit develop side-by-side. Nicotine dependence is an symptom of the addiction, but not the underlying reason. If you're determined to stop smoking, substituting smoking cigarettes using nicotine patches, or a cup of coffee won't be able help as these methods don't address the triggers which trigger the urge to smoke at all in the first place.

The desire for"nicotine "buzz" has been a typical reason for people who smoke, but the desire for stimulation that nicotine gives is usually present before the addiction. This is why many have discovered that switching to coffee can be enough to get rid of the habit. Coffee is a totally different chemical and will not eliminate your dependency of nicotine. What it does however, is to combat the psychological trigger that led you to turn to cigarettes initially, and offer you the satisfaction in getting "buzzed" and in a healthier manner.

But, many smokers have discovered it is the case that triggers for them have nothing to have to do with the chemical properties of cigarettes. For many people, smoking "smoke breaks" gave a sense of regularity to their lives and also a chance to interact with smokers around the world and even an excuse to get out for a short time each day. For them who smoke, anything from an easy walk, to a short workout to taking a break on social media are effective substitutes for smoking cigarettes that allow them to attain the structural or social benefits that they previously received from smoking cigarettes.

Whatever your routine is the two examples below show why understanding the cues you are using is essential for successful transformation of habits. Understanding the cue will assist you in understanding the motivation behind it. Sure, you'll feel some euphoria when you smoke a cigarette however, perhaps the thing that turned it into an addiction was the opportunity to talk to your colleague. When you're trying to stop smoking, a cigarette Nicorette may help you get rid of the nicotine craving but it's not enough to meet your need of social interactions. As long as that need remains unsatisfied and satisfied, you'll be tempted to smoke cigarettes whenever you feel yourself alone. For this reason, sending a text message to with a friend or using social media may be a great alternative which you're able to keep up over time. Maybe you could set a goal to call your family or friends whom you'd like to connect with every time you feel you craving a smoke. This replacement habit satisfy the social benefits you used to get from smokingcigarettes, but it can help you attain other goals socially related to having a more positive relationship with your family members or connecting with old friends.

However effective your new routine may be It's still important to select a method that you are confident will work. If you don't think you'll be able to overcome your habits, then you'll begin to sabotage yourself by feeling self-doubt. Keep in mind that those who are confident and relaxed have greater reserves of motivation and willpower that those who aren't. If you are doubtful of your capability to make a change and change, the more likely you are to fall back into old habits.

It's the reason why striving towards a particular target can be such an effective motivator. Some people have gone so in the direction of setting their own reward system in order to encourage them to keep with their new habits. For instance, if you're trying to substitute the evening TV viewing by jogging instead it might be beneficial to install a step-tracking application on your smartphone that tracks the number of miles you run. After you've completed the number of miles you need you can reward yourself with the purchase of a trip, holiday or some other reward for adhering to the new routine.

Conclusion

Thank you for buying this book!

I hope this book is useful to see how easy it is introduce new habits to your routine that can alter your life for good. Your perception of the world will depend on your. If you change your habits to improve your life increase the likelihood that your life will be more positive and joyful. It's true that stress plays a significant role in our modern world however it is your responsibility to discover how to alter your mental attitude and improve the quality of your interactions, your perception of the world, your faith and ultimately your overall happiness. If you are feeling negative anytime within your life, take this as a signal to tell you that there is something wrong in the overall balance of your life. Utilize it as an opportunity to establish an actionable habit into its place. People are often enthralled with life and assume that things will get better. But, as we've explained to you, at times the only way to get things under control is to make changes yourself.

The next step is to build upon the positive habits you have developed. ones. Read the book and learn on various aspects that you live in. Note down the kinds of behaviors you could incorporate to enhance your life to make it more enjoyable and then build them on top of the habits you already are using. Every habit is created out of repetition. So when you keep on including these positive behaviors into your daily routine it will result in positive effects on the way you view your life. You should be able to engage throughout your life. If you don't think of yourself as being creative, you're missing the obvious. Your creativity might lie in coming up with imaginative solutions to issues. Creativity isn't just about making things or drawing images. It can be found in all aspects that you live in. Use a notebook to think about ways that you are creative . Then, recognize and embrace your own creative side.

Discover something new. This is always beneficial, even if the new thing you're doing is just learning one word per day in the language you are not familiar with It all will result in using the brain cells that deal with learning, which is a way to open new possibilities to enhance your life. One woman I spoke to said that she wasn't very creative. Yet, when I spoke to her children it was revealed that she was creative , but she had shut off her capacity to be creative, by giving it a different name. Making a meal for children to enjoy was as imaginative as creating paintings in oil. She used clever methods to disguise the vegetables she did not like, and nobody believed she was a genius and creative, but she wasn't. Once she realized her own creative potential and rediscovered her passion for creativity, life was more satisfying for her.

We often don't see our own potential since we think of our lives as small. Be honest. Consider the things you've always thought of doing and incorporate them into your own life. It is possible to blame a lack of funds. It is possible to blame a insufficient the time. However, if would really like to incorporate something into your daily routine it is possible to take a shot at the stars by adjusting a few aspects of yourself that allow you more flexibility. If you shut yourself off to your own potential you restrict your possibilities.

In this book, we've covered every aspect of life since there are habits that exist throughout all areas. It is possible to have more friends and more enjoyable interactions with your friends. You can be able to enjoy your job more than you are currently simply by adopting positive reinforcement ways of living that make your life more enjoyable. It is possible to change your threshold to be patient or compassionate and most importantly you can be extremely grateful for the life you live by examining what you do every day as an extension of your life and what it could mean to you. You can take these practices and alter your life in a way that is beyond your imagination. You are obligated to become the best you can be. Reading the book over and over will allow you to reach that goal within the 30 days we promise to change your life.

Thank you for your kind words and best wishes!

www.ingramcontent.com/pod-product-compliance
Lightning Source LLC
Chambersburg PA
CBHW060328030426
42336CB00011B/1254